Psychology Revivals

The Depths of the Soul

Wilhelm Stekel was an Austrian physician and psychologist and one of Freud's earliest followers. This title, originally published in 1921, was the author's favourite of his own work. In the preface he says: 'It was written in the beautiful years in which the first rays of analytic psychognosis penetrated the darkness of the human soul.' Covering a variety of topics he takes a psychoanalytic look into *The Depths of the Soul*.

The Depths of the Soul

Psycho-analytical studies

William Stekel

LONDON AND NEW YORK

First published in 1921
by Kegan Paul, Trench, Trubner & Co., Ltd

This edition first published in 2014 by Routledge
27 Church Road, Hove BN3 2FA

and by Routledge
711 Third Avenue, New York, NY 10017

Routledge is an imprint of the Taylor & Francis Group, an informa business

Publisher's Note
The publisher has gone to great lengths to ensure the quality of this reprint but points out that some imperfections in the original copies may be apparent.

Disclaimer
The publisher has made every effort to trace copyright holders and welcomes correspondence from those they have been unable to contact.

ISBN: 978-1-138-01865-5 (hbk)
ISBN: 978-1-315-77960-7 (ebk)
ISBN: 978-1-138-01870-9 (pbk)

THE DEPTHS OF THE SOUL

PSYCHO-ANALYTICAL STUDIES

BY

DR. WILLIAM STEKEL

AUTHORIZED TRANSLATION
BY
DR. S. A. TANNENBAUM

LONDON
KEGAN PAUL, TRENCH, TRUBNER & CO., LTD.
BROADWAY HOUSE, 68-74 CARTER LANE, E.C.
1921

PREFACE

An old proverb says that every parent loves the ugly duckling most. My book, *The Depths of the Soul*, was, from its beginning, my favourite. It was written in the beautiful years in which the first rays of analytic psychognosis penetrated the darkness of the human soul. The reader may find between the lines the exuberant joy of a discoverer. First impressions are the strongest. It is an unfortunate fact that subsequent impressions lack the vividness, the intensity, the warmth, and the colours of the first emotions.

The great success of this book in many foreign languages has given me incalculable pleasure, because it has served to confirm my own blind love. No other book has brought me so many friends from far and near.

I am happy that my friend Dr. Tannenbaum has devoted his knowledge of the art of translation to my favourite child, and I hope that this translation will bring me many new English friends.

THE AUTHOR.

CONTENTS

THE SECOND WORLD

To poets it is a familiar world. The ordinary mortal wanders about in its wonderful gardens as if he were blind; he lives in it without knowing it. He does not know where the real world stops and where the fantasy world begins. In the treadmill of grey day the invisible boundaries between these two worlds escape him.

The second world! What would our life be without it? What a vale of tears would this globe be were it not for this heaven on earth!

The reader probably guesses what I mean. All of us, the poorest and the richest, the smallest and biggest, rarely or never find contentment in our daily routine. We need a second sphere, a richer life, in which we may dream of everything that is denied us in the first sphere. Ibsen called this "The Great Life-Lie." But is it always a lie? Did not Ibsen go too far with this characterization? Who could doubt that this lie is not one of those eternal truths that is so incorporeal that we cannot grasp it, so colourless that we cannot see it, so formless that we cannot describe it.

The child finds its second world in play. The little duties of everyday life are for it only unnecessary interruptions in its play in the second world. Here the child's fantasy has ample room. It is a soldier, king, and robber, cook, and princess; it rides through a wide world on steaming express trains, it battles courageously with dragons and giants, it snatches the treasures of the earth from their guardian dwarfs, and even the stars in the heavens are not beyond its reach in its play. Then comes the powerful dictum called education and snatches the child out of its beloved second world and compels it to give heed to the first world and to learn things necessary to it in its actual life. The child learns of obligations and submits unwillingly to the dictates of its teachers. The first world is made up of duties. The second world knows no duties; it knows only freedom and unrestrained freedom of thought. This is the root of the subsequent great conflict between feelings and duties. In our childhood we find duties a troublemaker who interferes with our playing; this childish hostility continues with us all through life. Our vocation, the sphere of our duties, can never wholly satisfy us. It is our first world; and even though we seem to accept it wholly, a little remnant of this hostility remains and this constitutes a part of our second world.

Primitive people find their second world in religion. From their primitive fears for the preservation of their lives they flee to their gods, whom they love and fear, punish and reward. The same thing is true of all those simple souls whom culture has not robbed of their religious belief. To them religion is the second world which gives them rich consolation and solace for the pains of the first world. In his book "Seelenkunde," Benedict attributes anarchism to an absence of consolatory life-lies. He says: "Our free-thinking times have stopped up this source and it is the duty of society to create a consoling life-truth, otherwise that psychic inner life which hoards up bitter hatred will not cease."

The more highly developed a person's mind is, the more complicated is his second world. People often express surprise at the fact that so many physicians devote themselves passionately to music or the other fine arts. To me it seems very simple. All day long they see life in its most disagreeable aspects. They see the innocent sufferings, the frightful tortures which they cannot relieve. They look behind the curtain of the "happy family"; they wade through all the repellant and disgusting filthiness of this petty world, and they would have to become dull and non-partisan animals did they not have their second world.

There is first of all music, which is so dear to all of us because it is an all-embracing mother which absorbs all the emotions of hatred, anger, love, envy, fear, and despair, and fuses them all into one great rhythm, into one great vibrating emotion of pleasure. On its trembling waves the thoughts of the poor tortured human soul are borne out into the darkness of uncomprehended eternity and the eternally incomprehensible.

Then there is literature. We open a book and at once we are transported into the second world of another ego, a world which in a few minutes becomes our own. Happy poets, who have been endowed with the gift of saying what they see, of giving form to what they dream, of freeing themselves from their energies, of abreacting their secret sufferings and of making others happy by opening up to them a second world!

Then there are the thousand and one forms of play; sports and in fact everything that tears us away from our daily grind. What is the lottery ticket to the poor wage-earner but an instalment on the pleasures of the second world, or the purchased right of joyous hope?

There is the devotion to clubs and fraternal associations. The henpecked husband flees wrathfully to his club where he can freely and fearlessly launch all those fine argumentative speeches which he has to suppress at home. Here he can rule, here he can play the role of the independent master. For many thousands the club is nothing more than an opportunity to work off their energies, to get rid of unused emotions and to play that role which life in the first sphere has denied them.

And thus everyone has his second world. One who does not have it stands on the level of animals, or is the happiest of the happy. By happiness I mean the employment of one's energies in the first sphere. There is a wide gulf between happiness and the consciousness of happiness. The consciousness of happiness is such a fugitive moment that the poorest wage-slave in his second world can be happier than the truly happy who does not happen to be thinking of his happiness. Happiness is like the possession of a beautiful wife. If we are in danger of losing her we tremble. Before we have obtained her and in moments of jealousy we guard her possession as fortune's greatest gift. But in the consciousness of undisturbed possession can we be saying to ourselves every second: I possess her, I am happy? No! no! Happiness is the greatest of all life's lies and one who has had least of it may be the happiest in his second world.

Rose-coloured hope! Queen of all pleasurable emotions, our all-preserving and all-animating goddess! You are the sovereign of the second world and beckon graciously the unhappy weeping mortal who in the first world sees the last traces of you disappear.——

Marital happiness depends very largely upon whether the two spheres of the couple partly overlap or touch each other at a few points. In the first world they must live together. But woe if the second world keeps them asunder! If the two spheres touch each other even only in one point and have only one feeling tangent between them, that will bring them closer together than all the cares and the iron constraint of the first world. Women know this instinctively, especially during the period of courtship. They enthuse about everything over which the lover enthuses; they love and hate with him and want to share everything with him. Beware, you married women, of destroying your husband's second world! If after the day's toil he soothes his tired nerves in the fateful harmonies of Beethoven, do not disturb his pious mood; enthuse with him, do not carry the petty cares and the vulgar commonplaces of life into the lofty second world. Do you understand me, or must I speak more plainly? Do not let him go alone on his excursions into the second world! A book that he reads alone, understands alone, enjoys alone, may be more dangerous to you than the most ardent glances of a wanton rival. Art must never become the man's second world. No! It must become the child of both the lovers if the beats of their souls are to be harmonious.

True friendship is so lofty, so exalting, because it is dependent upon a congruence of the second spheres. Love is a linking of the first worlds and if it is to be permanent it must journey forth into the second world. Genuine friendship is born in the second world and affects the first world only retroactively.

The second world need not necessarily always be the better world even though to its possessor it may appear to be the more beautiful and the more desirable. Rarely enough it is the supplement to the first world but frequently the contrast and the complement to it. Pious chaste natures may often give their coarser instincts undisturbed expression in the second world. Day-dreams are frequently the expression of life in the second world. But on careful analysis even the dreams of the night prove to be an unrestricted wallowing in the waters of the second world. Dreams are usually wish fulfillments, but in their lowest levels we find the wishes of the second world which are only rarely altered by unconscious thought processes.

One who dreams during the day flies from the first world into the second. If he fails to find his way back again into the first world his dreams become delusions and we say that he is insane. How delicate are the transitions from sanity to insanity! Inasmuch as all of us live in a second world, all of us are insane at least a few seconds every day. What distinguishes us from the insane is the fact that we hold in our hands the Ariadne thread which leads us out of the labyrinth of thoughts back into the world of duties.

It is incredible how happy an insane person can be. Proudly the paranoid hack writer marches up and down in his pitiful cell. Clothed in rags, he is king and commands empires. His cot is a heavenly couch of eiderdown;

his old dilapidated stool is a jewel-bedecked throne. The attendants and the physicians are his servants. And thus in his delusion he is what he would like to be.

The world is only what we think it; the "thing itself" is only a convention of the majority. A cured maniac assured me that the period of his insanity had been the happiest in his life. He saw everything through rose-coloured glasses and the awful succession of wild thoughts was only a succession of intensely pleasurable emotions. Obviously those, on the other hand, who suffer from melancholia and delusions of inferiority are the unhappiest creatures. The invalid who thinks himself made of glass trembles apprehensively for his life with every step. The unhappy experiences of the first world have become so fixed in his brain that they follow him into the second world and transform even this into their own image.

Every impression in our life affects our soul as if it were made of wax and not one such impression can be lost. That we forget so many impressions is due to the fact that we have repressed them out of our consciousness. Repression is a protective device but at the same time a cause for many serious nervous disorders. A painful impression, an unpleasant experience in the first or the second world, is so altered as to be unrecognizable in consciousness. As a reaction to this serious nervous disturbances, especially hysterical alterations of the psyche, may occur,—conditions which can be cured only by tracing out the dark pathways of the repressed emotions and reintroducing them into consciousness. They are conjured out of the dark realm of the unconscious into the glaring light of day and, lo! the ghosts vanish for all time and with them all those unpleasant symptoms which have so exercised the physician's skill.

If the psychotherapeutist is to fulfill his difficult task he must acquaint himself with the patient's second world even more thoroughly than with the first. And so, too, a judge ought never to pronounce sentence without first having thoroughly penetrated the second world of the condemned. In that world are the roots of good and evil in human life. In his "Crime and Punishment" Dostoyevsky's genius shows in a masterly way the relationship between the two worlds of a criminal. And so, too, Tolstoy, in his "Resurrection," in an endeavour to enlist our sympathies in her behalf, describes the second world of a courtesan. It is her life-lie that she makes all the men in her embrace blessed. And in sooth, a spark of truth seems to slumber in this life-lie.

Physicians, judges, lawyers, and ministers ought all to have a thorough training in psychology. Not psychology in the sense of that school philosophy which flourishes in theoretical phraseology and in theoretical facts remote from the green tree of life. Life can learn only from life. One who knows the secrets of the second world will not be surprised by any happenings that the day may bring forth. He will understand the weaknesses of the great and the strength of the small.

He will see virtue and vice coalesce in one great stream whose murky waters will flow on into unknown regions.

GRATITUDE AND INGRATITUDE

Very few people perceive the ridiculous element in the frequent complaints about the wickedness of human nature. "Human beings are ungrateful, false, untrustworthy," and so forth. Yes, but we are all human. We ought, therefore, logically speaking, complain: "We human beings are ungrateful, we are false, we are untrustworthy." But naturally this requires a measure of self-knowledge that is seldom to be found in those bearing the vesture of humanity. Let us make a modest beginning; let us try to look truth in the face. Let us not put ourselves on a pinnacle above the others till we know how high or low we ourselves stand.

We like to deceive ourselves, and, above all, not to see our faults. That is the most prevalent of all weaknesses. We look upon ourselves not only as cleverer but also as better than all others. We forget our faults so easily and divide them by a hundred, whereas our virtues are ever present to our mind and multiplied by a thousand. To himself everybody is not only the first but also the wisest and the best of mortals. That is why we complain about the ingratitude of our fellow-men, because we have forgotten all the occasions on which we proved ungrateful,—in exactly the same manner in which we manage wholly to forget everything calculated to awaken painful emotions in ourselves.

The complaint about man's ingratitude is as old as the history of man himself. The Bible, ancient legends, the folk-songs, and the proverbs of all nations, ancient and modern, bewail man's ingratitude. It is "the touch of nature that makes the whole world kin." A trait that is so widely distributed, investing the egoist with the glory of supreme worldy wisdom and branding the altruist as half a fool, must be founded deep in the souls of men. It must be an integral part of the circumstances conditioning the life of the individual. It must send its roots down into the unconscious where the brutal instincts of primal man consort with humanity's ripened instincts.

But if ingratitude is a genuinely (psychologically) established fact then we must be able to determine the dark forces that have it in them to suppress the elementary feeling of gratitude. For even to the most casual observation it is apparent that the first emotion with which we re-act to a kindness is a warm feeling of recognition, gratitude. So thoroughly are we permeated by it that it seems impossible ever to withhold this gratitude from our benefactor, let alone repay him with ingratitude. The first reaction with which the human soul requites a kind deed is a firm purpose "ever" to be grateful therefor. But purpose, "the slave to memory," is only the puffed sail that drives the boat until the force of the storm and the weakness of the rudder compel a different course. So, too, the intent to prove grateful is driven about fitfully by the winds of life. Of course, not at once. It requires the lapse of a certain latency period ere gratitude is converted to ingratitude. In the beginning the feeling of gratitude reigns supreme. Slowly it grows fainter and fainter, is inaudible for a time, then on suitable occasions is heard again but ever more faintly. After a while, quite unawares, ingratitude has taken its place. All those pleasurable emotions that have accompanied gratitude have been transformed into their opposites: love into hatred, attraction into aversion, interest into indifference, praise into censure, and friendship into hostility.

How does this come about? Where lie the sources of these hidden streams that drive the wheels of our emotions?

We pointed out at the very beginning that everybody regards himself as the wisest, the best, and the most capable of men. Our weaknesses we acknowledge very reluctantly. A losing chess-player is sure to say in ninety-nine out of a hundred instances: "I did not play this game well." The opponent's superiority is always denied; defeat is attributed to a momentary relaxation of the psychic tension, to carelessness, to some accident, etc. And if an individual is compelled to admit another's superiority, he will do so only with reference to some one point. He will always make reservations leaving himself some sphere of activity in which he is king. That constitutes a man's secret pride: the sphere in which he thinks he excels all others. This self-consciousness, this exaggerated apperception of the ego is a natural basis of life, a protective device of the soul which makes life bearable, which makes it easier to bear our fardels and endure the pricks of destiny, and which compensates us for the world's inadequate recognition of us and for the failure of our efforts which must inevitably come short of our intentions. "The paranoid delusion of the normal human being," as Philip Frey aptly named it, is really the individual's "fixed idea" which proves him to be in a certain sense pathologic and justifies the opinion that the whole world is a great madhouse.

This exaggerated self-consciousness manifests itself with pathological intensity especially in these times. The smaller the individual's share in the real affairs of the world is, the more must his fantasy achieve so as to magnify this function and have it appear as something of vital importance. In those cases in which individuality is crushed, a hypertrophied delusion of greatness is developed. Everyone thinks himself important, everyone is indispensable, everyone thinks himself an important power in the play and interplay of forces. Our era has created the type of the "self-made man." Everyone is willing to be indebted only to himself, his qualifications, his power of endurance, his energy, his individual efforts for his achievements. "By his own efforts"—so runs the much-abused phrase,—does each one want to get to the top.

All want it—but how few really make it come true! Who can know to-day what is his own and what another's? Who knows how much he had to take before he was able to give anything? But no one wants to stop for an accounting. Each one wants to owe everything to himself.

Something of this is in everyone of us. And this brings us to the deepest root of ingratitude. The feeling of being indebted to another clashes with our self-confidence; the unpleasant truth contrasts sharply with the normal's deep-rooted delusions of greatness. In this conflict of emotions there is only an either . . . or. *Either* once for all to renounce this exaggerated self-consciousness, *or* to forget the occasion for gratitude, to repress this painful memory, to let the ulcerous wound on the proud body of the "ego" heal to a scar. (The exceptions that prove the rule in this matter, too, we shall consider later.)

The first road that assures us eternal gratitude is chosen only by those who by the "bludgeonings of fate" have been wholly stunned, who are life-weary,—feel themselves goaded to death,—the wholly crushed. These unfortunates no longer need the play of their hidden psychic forces. The need of the body has strangled the cry of the soul. These are grateful, grateful from conviction, grateful from necessity. Their dreams are veritable orgies of benefactions. For them the benefactor is the deliverer from bodily torment. They see "dead souls" whom everyone who so desires may purchase.

But one who has not for ever renounced the fulfillment of his inmost longings will rarely be capable of gratitude. His ego resents being indebted to anyone but himself. But this ego will never permit itself to face the naked brutal fact of its ingratitude. It seeks for causes and motives, for justification. In this case the proverb again proves true: "seek and you shall find," the kindness is scrutinised from every side till a little point is found which reveals a bit of calculating egoism from which the kindness takes on a business aspect. And what human action does not permit of many interpretations? Our self-preservation impulse then chooses the interpretation that suits us best, the interpretation that relieves us of the oppressive feeling of gratitude. Such is the first step in the transformation of gratitude into ingratitude. Rarely does the matter rest there. Usually it requires also a transformation of the emotion into its opposite ere the galling feeling of gratitude can be eradicated. What execrable wretches would we not appear even to ourselves if we could not work out reasons for the changes in our feelings? And so we convert the good deed into a bad one; if possible, we discover stains and blots in our benefactor's present life or pursuits that can blacken the spotlessness of his past. Not until we have done this are we free from the oppressive feeling of gratitude. Thus, with no further reason for being grateful left, our personal pride survives unshaken, the bowed ego again stands proudly erect.

This explanation of the psychology of ingratitude draws the veil from a series of remarkable phenomena which we pass by in our daily life without regard or understanding. We shall cite only a few instances from the many at our disposal: the ingratitude of servants and all subordinates,—a species of ingratitude that is so obvious that if an exception occurs the whole world proclaims it as an exception; the ingratitude of pupils to the teacher to whom they owe all (this explains the common phenomenon that pupils belittle the scientific attainments of the teacher,—a phenomenon that may almost be designated "the pupil's neurosis"); the deep hatred with which artists regard those of their predecessors to whom they are most indebted; the tragedy of the distinguished sons whose fathers paved the way for them; the great injustice of invalids towards the physicians to whom they owe their lives; the historic ingratitude of nations to their great leaders and benefactors; the stubborn ignoring of the living great ones and the measureless overvaluation of the dead; the perpetual opposition to whatever administration may be in power, whence is derived a fragment of the psychology of discontent; the quite frequent transformation of a friendship into its opposite.

Verily, one who counts upon gratitude is singularly deficient in knowledge both of human nature and of his own nature. In this connection, we must consider also the fact that owing to an excessive overvaluation of the performance of our most obvious duties, we demand gratitude even when there is no reason for expecting it. I refer to only one example: Is there not an obvious obligation on parents to provide to the best of their ability for the child that they have brought into the world? Notwithstanding this we daily preach to our children: "You must be grateful to us for all that we do for you, for your food, your clothes, your education." And is it not a fact that this insistence upon the duty of children to be grateful begets the opposite: ingratitude? Should we not rather strive to hold our children with only one bond, *love?*

Let us be just and also admit that really grateful human beings are to be found; persons whom life has not wearied and who lose none of their dignity though they are grateful. These are the spiritually pre-eminent individuals who have forced themselves to the recognition of the fact that no one is an independent unit, that our valuation of ourselves is false, individuals who have succeeded, by the aid of psychoanalytic self-knowledge, to reduce the normal person's delusional greatness to the moderation warranted by reality.

Such persons are grateful because their valuation of themselves is fed by other springs. The knowledge of the frailties of humanity in general compensates them for the failing of the human in the individual. The greatest number of grateful persons will be found in the ranks of the geniuses, whereas talented persons are generally addicted to ingratitude. Genius can easily be grateful inasmuch as the frank recognition of one's weaknesses and the secret knowledge of one's achievements do not permit the suppression of the greatness of others. One who has so much to give need not be ashamed to have accepted something. And more especially as he knows with certainty that in life everyone must accept. . . .

Truly great men are notably modest. Modesty is the knowledge of one's own shortcomings. Vanity, the overvaluation of one's endowments. Gratitude is the modesty of the great ; ingratitude the vanity of the small. Only those are grateful who really have no occasion for being so. A genuine benefactor finds his thanks in good works. In dealing with this theme one must think of Vischer's verses :—

> " If poison and gall make the world bitter,
> And your heart you would preserve ;
> Do deeds of kindness ! and you will learn
> That doing good rejoices."

UNPACKING ONE'S HEART

The average human being finds it helpful to free himself from his impressions by "pouring out his heart" to someone. Like a sponge, the soul saturates itself; like a sponge, it must be squeezed dry before it can fill itself up again. But now and then it happens that the soul cannot rid itself of its impressions. Such persons, we say, are soul-sick and we recognise those who suffer from soul-sickness by the fact that they sedulously shun new impressions. Every disease of the soul rests ultimately upon a secret.

Children exhibit in clear and unmistakable ways the reactions of their elders. In the presence of a secret they behave exactly as the normal person ought to behave. They cannot keep it to themselves. I recall very distinctly that as a child I was unable to sit a quarter of an hour without speaking. Repeatedly my parents promised me large rewards if I would sit a quarter of an hour without asking them a question or making some remark. The promised reward was increased from day to day because I never was quiet for more than half of the allotted period. But the obligation to keep a "secret" was even more discomforting to me.

On one occasion my brother was to be given a silver watch for his birthday. For three days I went about oppressed and restive as if something was seriously amiss. I prowled around him, watching him intently with suppressed excitement, so that he finally noticed my strange behaviour and demanded to know what I wanted. On the day before his birthday I could contain myself no longer and while we were at dinner I burst out with, "Oh, you don't know that you are going to get a silver watch to-morrow!"

All children are, doubtless, like that. A secret is to them an unbearable burden. When the time comes that they must keep some matters secret from their parents because an inexplicable shyness makes them ashamed to talk everything over with them freely, they change their attitude towards their parents and seek out a companion of their own age, some friend with whom they can discuss their secret.

Adults are really as little capable of going about with a secret as children are. It tortures and oppresses them like a heavy burden; and they are happy to rid themselves of it one way or another. If they cannot speak of it openly and frankly then they do so in some hidden, secret, or symbolic way. I could cite numerous illustrations of this but shall content myself with only one. A woman who had committed the unpardonable sin became troubled with a remarkable compulsive action. She was continually washing her hands. Why? Because she was dominated by the feeling that she was dirty, that she had become unclean. She could not tell any one in the world what she had done ; she would have loved to say to her husband and to the whole household : " Do not touch me ! I am impure, unclean, an outcast ! " She had found a means of making this confession, but she did so in a form which only the expert can understand. At every appropriate and inappropriate occasion she washed her hands. If she was asked why she washed her hands she answered, " Because they are not clean." Such symbolic actions are extremely common and constitute a kind of " speech without words " (to use Kleinpaul's apt words). But a symbolic action is nothing but a substitution, a compromise between antagonistic psychic currents. It bears, however, no comparison with the freeing effect of pouring one's heart out in words to a person, a confidant one can trust.

We know from the statements of convicts that nothing is so hard to bear in prison as the impossibility of " getting things off their chest." And why is it that when touring foreign countries we so readily make friends with our townspeople whom we happen to meet, though at home we are quite indifferent to them ? Because they furnish the opportunity for a good talk, because to a certain extent they become receptacles into which we may empty our soul's accumulations. The profound yearning that we all harbour for friendship, for a sympathetic soul, emanates from the imperative need for pouring our hearts out. By means of a good talk of this sort, we " abreact," or throw off a part of our pent-up excitement. Children are much more fortunate than we in this regard. How easily they find a friend! The first-best play-fellow becomes a friend and confidant within half an hour. But for us grown-ups the matter is much more difficult. Before we can take any one into our confidence, take him to our bosom, he must satisfy certain social and ethical requirements. But in reality we disclose only the surface and retain our most oppressive secrets deep down at the bottom of the soul unless a sudden storm of passion overcomes us; then the sluice-gates burst open and the dammed up waters pour out in turgid torrents, carrying everything before them.

The tremendous power of the Roman Catholic Church is even to-day due to the fact that it enables its members to confess their most secret sufferings from time to time and to be absolved. Dr. Muthmann calls attention to the fact that suicides are most frequent in Protestant countries, and least frequent among Roman-Catholic peoples, and he thinks that this is to be attributed to the influence of the confessional, one of the greatest blessings for numberless people.

The psycho-analytic method of treating nervous diseases has not only made the incalculable benefit of confession its own but has united with it the individual's spiritual education inasmuch as it teaches him how to know himself and to turn his eyes into the darkest depths of his soul. But there is also a kind of speaking out that is almost equivalent to confession—self-communion. That is, one's communings with oneself. For, as Grillparzer says, every heart has its secrets that it anxiously hides even from itself. Not all of us know how to detect such secrets. The poet has this gift. As Ibsen beautifully says: "To live is to master the dark forces within us; to write is to sit in judgment on ourselves." But only a poet is able to sit in judgment on his own soul. Not every person has the capacity for self-communion. Most of the diseases of the soul depend upon the peculiar mechanism that Freud has called "repression." This "repression" is a semi-forgetting of displeasing impressions and ideas. But only a half-forgetting. For a part of the repressed idea establishes itself in some disguised form as a symptom or as some form of nervous disease. In these cases the psychotherapeutist must apply his art and teach the invalid to know himself.

Goethe knew the value of confession. He reports that he once cured a Lady Herder by confession. On September 25th, 1811, he wrote to Mrs. Stein: "Last night I wrought a truly remarkable miracle. Lady Herder was still in a hypochondriacal mood in consequence of the unpleasantnesses she had experienced in Carlsbad, especially at the hands of her family. I had her confess and tell me everything, her own shortcomings as well as that of the others, in all their minutest details and consequences, and at last I absolved her and jestingly made her understand that by this ritual these things had now been disposed of and cast into the deeps of the sea. Thereupon she became merry and is really cured." Here we have the basic principles of modern psychotherapy. Unconsciously, by virtue of the hidden power of his genius, the poet accomplished what modern therapeutists also attempt.

Nietzsche, too, fully understood the value of confession. We are accustomed at once to associate with Nietzsche the concept of the Antichrist. That he has accurately conceived the essence of the true priest he shows in his description of the priestly temper in his book, "The Joyful Wisdom." He says, "the people honour a wholly different kind of man, . . They are the mild, earnest, simple, and modest priestly natures . . . . before whom one may pour out one's heart with impunity, upon whom one may unload one's secrets, one's worries, and what's even worse." (The man who shares himself with another frees himself from himself; and one who has acknowledged, forgets.)

It would be impossible to state the value of confession more beautifully and more clearly. It will not be long ere this view which knocks commandingly at the door of science and which has already been productive of good will be generally accepted. It will not be long ere it will furnish us a deep insight into the genesis of the "endogenetic mental diseases," excepting, of course, those "exogenetic" maladies that follow some of the infectious diseases. We shall look upon the "endogenetic" diseases, even delusions, as a disturbance of the psychic circulation, and it will be our task to ascertain the causes that bring these maladies about.

There are numbers of substitutes which are equivalent to a kind of confessing to oneself. These are art, reading of newspapers, music, literature, and, least but not last, the theatre. The ultimate effect of a dramatic presentation depends, in reality, upon the liberation in us of affects that have been a long time pent up within us. It is not without good reason that humanity throngs to witness tragic plays during the performance of which it can cry to its heart's content. When the spectators are apparently shedding tears over the unhappy fate of a character on the stage they are really crying over their own pain. And the woman who laughs so heartily at the awkward clumsiness of a clown, that the tears run down her cheeks, is perhaps laughing at her husband, who, though she will not acknowledge it, appears to her just as stupid and clumsy; she is thereby excusing to herself her own sins which she has possibly committed only in fantasy. The theatre serves as a kind of confessional; it liberates inhibitions; awakens many memories, consoles, and perhaps renews in us hopes of secret possibilities as to whose fulfillment we have long since despaired.

We have become accustomed of late to suspect sex-motives behind friendship. Even if we accept the theory that these motives are present, but hidden in the unconscious, it is a far from adequate explanation for the longing for friendship. The unconscious sex-motive unquestionably co-operates in a significant measure in the choice of a friend. It may be the determining factor in what we call sympathy and antipathy, although it would have to be proved with regard to the latter, and the theme is deserving of separate consideration, for it is quite possible that our antipathies are only reactions to an excessive attraction and therefore are evidence of repression. Looked at from this point of view, sympathy and antipathy are one feeling, one affect, having in the former case a positive sign and in the latter a negative sign. This secret tendency may be the deciding factor in the choice of a friend. But the need for a friend surely is in direct relation to the need for confession.

It is customary to ridicule the Germans' passion for forming clubs, and societies of all kinds. But do these founders of fraternal associations seek for anything but an opportunity to fraternise, to have a good talk, something from which they are barred at home? The innumerable speeches that are delivered during the course of a year, and which are being poured out every second in an endless stream in some house at some meeting are apparently being spoken only for the benefit of the auditors. But every speech is a kind of relief to the speaker's "I," and people who have the craving to speak before the whole world are very often the keepers of a great secret which they must conceal from the world and which they are imparting in this indirect way in homœopathic doses. Just as a dye that is dissolved in a large quantity of fluid is so completely lost that the naked eye can detect no trace of it, so do occasional particles of the great secret which must forever remain hidden find their way into the elocutionary torrent.

LAZINESS

There are commonplace maxims which people go on repeating thoughtlessly, and in the light of which they determine their conduct without once stopping to consider whether the assumed truth, looked at in the light of reason, may not turn out to be a lie. We know, of course, that there are many "truths" which may under certain circumstances prove to be falsehoods. Everything is in a state of flux! Truth and falsehood are wave crests and wave troughs, an endless stream driving the mills of humanity.

Such notorious maxims as the following are trumpeted into our ears from the days of our youth: "Work makes life sweet"; "Satan finds some mischief still for idle hands to do"; "the life of man is three-score-and-ten, and if it has been a happy one it is due to work and striving." These truisms are beaten into us, drummed into us, and hammered into us from all sides; we hear them wherever we go, till finally we accept them, completely convinced.

And it is well that it is so. What would the world look like if everybody pressed his claim to laziness? Think of the hideous chaos that would ensue if the wheels of industry came to a stop!

The admonition to work has its origin in humanity's instinct of self-preservation. It does not spring from one's own needs but only from the needs of others. Apparently we all work for ourselves, but in reality we are always working for others. How very small is the number of those who do their work gladly and cheerfully! How very many give vent to their aversion to work by means of apparent dissatisfaction with their calling! And where can we find a man nowadays who is contented with his calling?

Let us begin our study of man with that period of his life in which he was not ashamed to show his impulses to the light of day, in which repression and education had not yet exerted their restraining influences,—in other words, let us begin with the observation of childhood. With astonishment we note, first, that the child's impulse to idleness is stronger than the impulse to work. Play is for a long time the child's idleness as well as its work. A gymnast who proudly swings the heaviest dumb-bells before his colleagues would vent himself in curses, deep if not loud, if he had to do this as work; the heavy-laden tourist who pants his way up steep mountain paths would curse his very existence if he had to travel these difficult trails in the service of mankind in the capacity of—let us say—letter-carrier; the card player who works in the sweat of his brow for hours in the stuffy café to make his thousand or ten thousand points would complain bitterly at his hard lot and at the cruelty of his employers if he had to do an equivalent amount of work in the office. Anything that does not bear the stamp of work becomes in the play-form recreation and a release from almost unbearable tyranny.

The child's world is play. Unwillingly and only on compulsion does it perform imposed tasks. (It would have even its education made a kind of play.) Many parents worry about this and complain that their children take no pleasure in work, seem to have no sense of duty, forget to do their school work, and have to be forced to do their exercises. Stupid parents! If they only stopped to think they would realise that this frank display of an impulse to laziness is a sign of their children's sanity. For we often enough observe the opposite phenomenon. Children who take their duties too seriously, who wake too early in the morning lest they should be late for school, who are always poring over their books, scorning every opportunity to play, are usually "nervous" children. Exaggerated diligence is one of the first symptoms of neurosis.

One who can look back upon his own childhood must admit that the impulse to indolence is stronger than any other childhood impulse. I recall how unwillingly I went to high-school. Once I read in a newspaper that a high-school had burned to the ground and that the pupils would not be able to go to school for several weeks. For days I and my friends were disappointed as we looked at our own grey school building that stood there safe and sound. Had it not burned down yet ? ! Were we not to have any luck at all ? !

Who is not acquainted with the little sadistic traits that almost all children openly manifest ? Such a sadistic motive was our secret hope that this or that teacher would get sick and we would be excused from attendance at school. What a joy once possessed the whole class when we discovered that the Latin teacher was sick just on the day when we should have had to recite in his subject ! That was a grand prize !

And how the child detests always being driven to work ! Always the same disagreeable questions : "Have you no lessons to do to-day ?" "Have you done all your lessons ?" The profoundest wish of all who do not yet have to provide for themselves is once to get a chance to be as lazy as their hearts might desire.

But we adults, too, who know the pleasure of work and of fulfilled obligations, long for idleness. For us, too, the vice of laziness is an exquisite pleasure. We find it necessary continually to overcome the tendency to laziness by new little resolutions. In the morning laziness whispers : stay a little longer in your warm bed ; it's so comfortable. Another few seconds and the sense of duty prevails over the desire for idleness. In the afternoon we would love to spend an hour in pleasant day-dreams. Work conquers this wish too. And with what difficulty we get out of the performance of some task in the evening! It is an everlasting conflict even though it is in most cases a subconscious conflict with the sweet seducer of mankind: laziness.

That is why the lawgivers have ordained days on which the urge for laziness may be gratified. These are called holidays. Religion has made of this right to laziness a duty to God. The more holidays a religion has, the more welcome must it appear to labouring humanity. That is why the various religious systems so readily take over one another's holidays. The Catholic Church appropriated ancient heathenish feasts, and Jews bow to the Sunday's authority just as the Christian does.

Persons who suppress the inclination to laziness get sick. Their nerves fail soon and their capacity for work suffers serious diminution. And then we say that they had overworked. Not at all infrequently illness is only a refuge in idleness, a defence against a hypertrophied impulse to work. This is frequently observable in persons afflicted with nervousness. They are unfit for work, waste themselves away in endless gloomy broodings, in bitter self-reproaches, and in hypochondriacal fears. They do not tire of repeatedly protesting how happy they would be if they could get back to work again.

But if their unconscious mental life is analyzed one discovers with astonishment that the greatest resistance to a cure is offered by their laziness, the fear of work. This is one of the greatest dangers for the nervous patient. If a neurotic has once tasted of the sweets of laziness it is a very difficult matter to get him to work again. All the varieties of fatigue "cramps" known to neurologists, *e.g.*, writer's cramp, pianist's cramp, violinist's cramp, typewriter's cramp, etc., are rebellions on the part of the tendency to laziness. A return to work is possible only if, in the absence of an actual organic malady, the psychic element we have called "refuge in disease" (q.v.) is taken into consideration and given due weight.

This reluctance to work is most frequently noticeable in the puzzling "traumatic neuroses," the so-called "accident or compulsion hysterias" in which the so-called "hunger for damages" plays the most important role. Since labourers have acquired the right to recover damages for accidental injuries, the number of traumatic neuroses has increased so tremendously that insurance companies can scarcely meet the claims. This is also true of the neuroses following railway and street car accidents. Only seldom can objective injuries be demonstrated in these cases. But notwithstanding this, the injured person becomes depressed, moody, sleepless, and utterly unfit for any work. Yet it would be very unjust to consider them simulators.

They are really sick. Their psychic make-up has suffered a bad shaking-up. The pleasure in work has suffered a rude shock because of the unconscious prospect of pecuniary "damages," *i.e.* of an opportunity for laziness. Repressed desires from childhood are re-animated. Why should you work, says the alluring voice of the unconscious, when you can lounge about and live on an income? Don't be a fool! Get sick like the others who loll about idly and need not work! And consciousness, in its weakness, takes no note of the conflict in the unconscious, is frightened by the unknown restlessness and sleeplessness and gets sick . . . It is an obstinate conflict between laziness and industry from which only too often the former emerges triumphant . . .

Finally, the need for laziness becomes overpowering in all of us from time to time. We long for a vacation. We want to recuperate from work. Well, there are a few sensible people. These go off into a corner somewhere and are as lazy as they can be. They lie in the grass and gaze at the heavens for hours; or they go fishing in some clear stream,—one of the best ways of wasting time; they sit in a rowboat, letting someone else do the rowing or just keeping the boat in motion with an occasional stroke. In this way day after day is spent in *dolce far niente* until one wearies of laziness and an intense longing for work fills one's whole being. Variety is the spice of life. Without idleness work loses its charm and value.

Others employ their vacation for new work. These are the eternally restless, industrious, indefatigable ones for whom idleness does not exist. The impulse to laziness which was once so strong, is suppressed and converted into its opposite. These are usually persons who had their fill of laziness in childhood and who thoroughly enjoyed their youth. (We may refer briefly to a few well-known instances of this: there was Charles Darwin who began to work only after he left college; Bismarck, whose student days were a period of riot and idleness; John Hunter was another striking example.)

These continue with their work even while they are on their vacation. They make work even of their visits to art galleries, museums, show-places, and of their breathless flying trips hither and thither. This is really not the kind of idleness that means a relaxation of tension. It's only a variation in the kind of impressions. A sea-voyage would be a compromise between the two antagonistic tendencies. That is why Englishmen prefer a sea-voyage to other forms of rest. On board ship a person must be lazy. He sits on deck and stares at the waves. The vastness of the sea stands between him and his work. He must be idle. Impressions fly by him; he does not have to go in search of them.

The right to laziness is one of the rights that

sensible humanity will learn to consider as something self-evident. For the time being we are still in conflict with ourselves. We shun the truth. We look upon laziness as something degrading. We still stand in too much awe of ourselves to be able to find the right measure. Our mothers' voices still ring in our ears : " Have you done your lessons ? "

THOSE WHO STAND OUTSIDE

I am at the Circus with my children. They are laughing and clapping their hands in glee. They are delighted with the grotesque antics of the stupid clown. In vain I try to kindle my own enthusiasm at theirs as a means of banishing the unpleasant feeling of being bored. The peculiar odour of a menagerie pervades the great building and brings back to me, by way of the obscure paths that connect our thoughts, memories of days long since dead. I am myself a child again, my cheeks hot and flushed, sitting in the topmost gallery at the Circus, as excited as if I were beholding the greatest of all earthly wonders.

It is just when one of the star attractions is being given. A skilled athlete is vaulting over very great obstacles. He leaps over ten men in a row, five horses, a little garden. His faultless dress-suit shows scarcely a wrinkle after this feat. This too must be counted among the advances made by modern art. In my boyhood days athletes still wore a gay uniform and "worked" in costume. To-day every juggler and prestidigitator is a pattern of a drawing-room gentleman. Some may be making a virtue of necessity and gladly escape the exhibiting of their none too handsome bodies.

These reflections are suddenly interrupted by a blare of noisy music. Everybody is excited, for this seems to indicate that the athlete's most wonderful trick is coming. True; something out of the ordinary is happening. Through a wide gate an old-fashioned comfortable, drawn by a weary nag, is brought into the arena and our valiant athlete leaps over horse and rider amidst the thunderous applause of the enthusiastic youngsters and of those of their elders who have remained children in spirit.

The easy-going driver turns his vehicle towards the exit. Again the portals open wide. Bands of bright daylight pour into the half-darkened amphitheatre. In the glare one catches sight, for a moment, of a little section of the life that swarms round about the fringe of the Circus. There is the soda-water vendor with his gay-coloured cart, a labourer, a few servant girls, and some twenty little children staring with big eyes eagerly into the darkness of the arena in the hope of catching a glimpse of all this magnificence.

I shall never forget the sight. Those children's eyes, opened so tremendously wide, longing to catch a bit of happiness! How they envy the fortunate ones sitting in here and beholding real fairy-tale wonders!

I lapse into a day-dream again. I too am one of those little ones standing out there; I count the richly-caparisoned horses that are being led in; for the twentieth time I read the large placard announcing an "élite performance"; I am so happy as the beautiful equestrienne passes right by me; the muffled sounds of the music penetrate to my ears; I hear the animated applause and the bravos. One thought possesses me: I must get in! Cost what it may, I must go in!

Oh, I could have committed a theft to enable myself to get in there and share in the applause! And I thought to myself, if I am ever a rich man I shall go to the Circus every day. How excitedly I go home then, talking about all the wonderful things I have seen, and how in my dreams all my wishes are realized—all these things take on a tangible shape before my mind's eye.

I note that it was the most beautiful period of my life, the time when I used to stand outside. In those days I still had a sense of the wonderful. There was a touch of secret magic about everything. Even dead things had a message for me. Before me was an endless wealth of possibilities; and there stretched before me kingdoms of the future over which my childish wishes flew like migratory birds.

Verily—happiness is only anticipating possibilities, denying impossibilities. Life is filled up with dreams of the future. What we know seems trivial when measured by the knowledge we would like to acquire. Possession kills desire; realization slays fantasy and transforms the wonderful into the commonplace.

All the beauty of this world lies only in the fantasies which reality can never approximate. The marvels of the present are seen only by those who stand outside.

Every time that one of the portals that had been locked from our youthful eyes opened, every time longing became fulfilment, we became one pleasure poorer and one disappointment richer. Only with the aid of the stilts supplied us by philosophy can we rise above the depressing disillusionment of experience. Or, in playing our part in the great drama of life, we cling to the one role we have studied and keep on repeating it to ourselves until we, too, almost believe it. Then we succeed again in seizing a fringe of the magnificent purple mantle with which we aspired to adorn our life.

Those outside see everything on a much larger scale, finer, and grander. That is why we envy others their possessions, their realities, their calling. Because we project the inevitable disappointments of life upon the thing that is readiest at hand—and that is unquestionably our vocation. Our wishes circle around others' possibilities.

Involuntarily an experience from my youth occurs to me. I had for the first time in my life made the acquaintance of a poet. He was a well-known lyrist of that day and his delightful verses had charmed me for years. He did not in any way come up to the ideal that I had conceived of what a poet ought to be. The edges of his eyelids were red, his face was commonplace, and he had a large paunch. The manner in which he drank his coffee disgusted me. A little coffee dripped down on his dirty grey beard and with the movements of his big upper jaw some cake crumbs danced up and down on his moustache.

And that was the poet who wrote those passionate little lyrics! Overcoming my disappointment, I entered into conversation with him and let him perceive something of my admiration. He was to be envied for possessing the gift of transforming his moods and experiences into works of art!

To my astonishment the poet began to describe with palpable resentment the shortcomings of his calling. If he had only become an honest craftsman ere he had devoted himself to writing! He was sick of the hard struggle. To be ever at loggerheads with the public, the critics, the publishers, and editors—those were the compensations of his calling. He envied me for being a phsyician. That's a great, a noble, an ideal calling. A physician can do something for humanity! If he were not too old he would at once take up the study of medicine. To mitigate the pains of an invalid is worth more than writing a hundred good lyrics!

In those days I was not a little proud of the profession I had chosen. The poet was only saying openly what I thought in secret. "The physician is mankind's minister." How often later on have I heard these and similar words which were calculated to add fuel to the flame of idealism.

Ye gods ! In real life how sad is the physician's lot ! Those outside cannot conceive it. The first thing to realize is the rarity of the instances in which the physician really snatches the victim from the clutches of Death ; how rarely he eliminates suffering ; how frequently, discouraged and bewildered, he fails to halt the ravages of disease. How his idealism makes him suffer ! He is painfully aware that the craftsman comes nearer to his ideals than the artist. He becomes familiar with man's limitless ingratitude and realizes that unless he is to go into bankruptcy he must adopt the "practical" methods of the business man. He is the slave of his patients, has no holidays, not a free minute in which he is not reminded of his dependance. He sees former colleagues and friends who have accumulated fortunes in business or in the practice of the law, whereas he has to worry about his future and, with but few exceptions, live from hand to mouth. But he must continue to play the role of the "idealistic benefactor" unless he is to lose the esteem of those who—stand outside.

Not long ago I read a fascinating description of a "sanatorium." How within its walls fear blanches the cheeks of the inmates, how Death lurks behind the doors, how even the physicians avoid speaking above a whisper and glide with solemn and noiseless steps through the house of pain! Very pretty and sentimental; but utterly false,—as false as the observations of a littérateur who stands outside can make it. From within the thing looks quite different! While the surgeon is scrubbing and sterilising his hands someone is telling the latest joke, the assistants converse lightly and merrily, not at all as if a matter of life and death were going to be decided in a few minutes. And it is well for the patient that it is so. The surgeon and the assistants need their poise; they must not be moved by timidity, fear, or sympathy—emotions which cloud the judgment. Where one needs all one's senses, there the heart must be silent. The public feels this instinctively. I have found that those physicians who practised their profession in a plain matter of fact way, as a business, were the most popular and the busiest. And, on the other hand, I know learned physicians who are all soul, whom everybody praises, esteems, heeds, but whom no one calls. The more highly the physician values his services, from a material point of view, the more highly he is regarded as an idealist, and vice versa.

That is how the idealism of the medical profession looks in real life. For many physicians their ideals are superfluous ballast. It often takes years before they find the golden mean between theory and practice, between ethics and hard facts.

And how is it with other vocations? In

every case in which it is possible to look behind the curtains it will appear that the envious natures of those who stand outside magnify the advantages and overlook the unpleasant aspects.

All life is a continual game between hope and fulfilment, between expectation and disappointment. And therein lies our good fortune—that we can still be deceived. Were we in possession of all truth and all knowledge, life would lose its value and its charm. Only because, in a certain sense, we all stand outside, because the fullness of life and "the thing itself" will continue to be a riddle, are we capable of continuing on our journey and approaching erectly the valley of death in which the shades dwell.

"Father, the show is over!" A child's sweet voice wakes me from my revery. Outside I again look at the children still standing there and staring with large, hungry eyes into the Circus . . .

WHAT CHILDREN ASPIRE TO

Who can say when the first wish opens its pious eyes in the child's soul? The child probably sleeps away the first few weeks of its existence without a single wish, all its behaviour being probably only manifestations of its inherited instincts. Suddenly the first wish awakens and the humanization of the little animal has begun. And with it begins the wild succession of desires, mounting ever higher and higher and finally aspiring even to the stars. How few of the things we have been dreaming of does life fulfil! Wish after wish, stripped of its purple mantle, sinks to the ground in a state of "looped and windowed raggedness," till the last wish of all—the longing for peace, eternal peace—puts an end to the play.

Our childhood wishes determine our destiny. They die only with our bodies. They go whirling through our dreams, are the masters of our unconscious emotions, and determine the resonance of the most delicate oscillations of our souls. It certainly seems worth while taking a closer look at these wishes. Unfortunately we are deprived of the best source of such knowledge: the observation of ourselves. For we forget so easily, and our earliest desires lie far behind us, hidden in thick mist. Only the dream pierces the thick veil and brings us greetings from a long forgotten era.

From the study of our children we can learn of only one kind of desire. A desire that can be easily observed, that the child betrays most easily in the games it plays.

"And what are you going to be?" That is the question one most often puts to children and which they very seldom allow to go unanswered.

Right here we must draw a distinction between boys and girls. The girl's first wish almost invariably betrays the influence of the sexual instinct. All little girls want to be "mothers"; some would be content with being "nurses." The phylogenetic law of the biologist applies also to desires. The desires of individual human beings reproduce the evolution of mankind in this regard. Just as, according to recent researches (Ament), the first speech attempts of children depict the primitive speech of man, so the first wishes of human beings depict the primitive wishes of humanity. Children's wishes may therefore be said to be the childhood wishes of humanity and to manifest unmistakeably the primitive instincts of the sexes.

The little girls want to become "mothers." They play with dolls, rocking, fondling, and petting them as if they were children. In this way they betray their most elemental qualification. My little daughter once said:

"Mother! I want to be a mother, too, some day and have babies." "I would be so unhappy if I could not have any babies!" Being asked whether she would not like to be a doctor, she replied: "Yes! I would love to be a doctor*! But only like mamma." That is, only the wife of a doctor.

In marked contrast with this is the fact that boys never wish to be fathers. That is: their fathers are often enough their ideals and they would like to be like them, to follow the same profession or vocation. But it's only a matter of vocation, not of family. I have never yet heard a boy express a wish for children. There is no doubt however, that there are boys who like to play with dolls and whose whole being has something of the feminine about it. They have feminine instincts. They love to cook and prefer to play with little girls. In the same way one also encounters girls who are described as "tomboys." These girls are wild, unruly, disobedient, boisterous, and like to play at soldiers and robbers. One cannot go wrong in concluding that a strong, perhaps even an excessive homosexual element enters into their psychic make-up. At any rate the biographies of homosexuals invariably make mention of these remarkable infantile traits. They are boys with female souls and girls with a masculine soul. Such boys may even manifest

*To understand what follows, the English reader should know that the German word for a female physician ("Doktorin") is also the title whereby a physician's wife is addressed.

various disguised indications of the instinct for race preservation.

The first stage of girlish wishes does not last long. Usually the process of repression begins rather early. The little girls notice that their desires are a source of mirth to their elders, and that their remarks evoke a kind of amused though embarrassed smirking in the people about them. So they begin to conceal and to repress the nature of their desires and to disclose only what is perfectly innocent. And they tell us they want to become "maids of all work," housewives. That does not sound as bad as wanting to be "mother." One can be a housewife without having children. As such they go marketing, manage the home, cook, order the servants about, etc. Then they are attracted by the splendours of being a cook. A cook is the goddess of sweets and delicacies and can cook anything she likes. On the same egoistic principle they then want to be store-keepers, proprietresses of candy stores, pastry shops, and ice cream parlours. As such they would have at their sole disposal all the sweets and delicious things a child's palate craves for. To possess a store in which one can sell these wonderful delicatessens and weigh them out to customers is one of the most ardent wishes of little girls.

Of course as soon as they go to school a new ideal begins to take possession of the childish soul. Up there in her tribunal sits the teacher, omniscient and omnipotent, invested with such authority that the parental authority pales into insignificance in comparison with it. Parental authority extends only to their children. But the teacher's! She has command over so many children! With sovereign munificence she distributes her gracious favours. She designates one child to act as "monitor" (oh, what exalted pre-eminence!); another may carry her books home; the third is permitted to restore the stuffed owl into the teacher's cabinet, or to clean the blackboard; the fourth has the rare privilege of being sent out to purchase the teacher's ham sandwich! And then there are the various punishments the teacher can inflict upon the children entrusted to her. Oh, it's just grand to be a teacher!

But, above all, the desire is to rule over many. Have I omitted to mention the "princess"? Incredible! Only few children are so naive as to betray this wish. But all would love to become "queens,"—ay, with all their hearts. The fairy tales are full of them. How the proud prince came and helped the poor girl mount his steed, saying: "Now you'll sit by me and be my Queen!" Innumerable Cinderellas in the north and in the south, in the east and in the west, sit at their compulsory tasks and dream of the prince who is to free them.

All have one secret dread: To be lost in the vast multitude. They want to accomplish something, want to stand out over the others. Vanity causes more suffering than ambition.

Soon, too soon, they learn that, these sober days princes do not go roaming about promiscuously as in the golden days of fairydom. But hope finds a way and soars on the wings of fantasy into the realm of the possible and yet wonderful. Are there not queens in the world of arts? Do they not rule like real queens their willingly humble subjects? Haven't they everything that a queen has: Gold, fame, honour, recognition, admiration, envy? Almost every girl goes through this stage. She wants to become a great artist. A prima donna such as the world has never yet known; a danseuse, who shall have the tumultuous applause of houses filled to the last seat; a celebrated actress whose finger-tips princes shall be permitted to kiss; a violinist whose bow shall sway the hearts of men more than the golden sceptre of a queen ever could.

This dream runs through the souls of all girls. It yearly furnishes the art dragon with thousands and thousands of victims. The happy parents believe it is the voice of talent crying imperatively to be heard. In reality it is only the beginning of a harassing struggle to get into the lime-light, a struggle that all women wage with in exhaustible patience as long as they live. And thus numberless amateur female dilettanti vainly contend for the laurel because they are so presumptuous as to try to transform a childish dream into a waking reality.

It is even more interesting to make a survey of what girls just past puberty do not wish to become. Not one wants to marry. (Reasons can always be found.) Not one wants to be an ordinary merchant's wife. And life then takes delight in bringing that to pass which seemingly they did not wish . . .

In boys the matter is more complicated. The sex-urge is not manifested so clearly in them as in girls. It requires great skill in the understanding of human conduct to discover in the games that boys play the symbolic connection with the natural impulses. It is remarkable that boys' earliest ideals are employments that are in some way or other related to locomotion. All little boys first want to be drivers, conductors, chauffeurs, and the like. Motion seems to fascinate the boy and to give him more pleasure than anything else. A ride in a street car or a bus which seems to us elders so obviously wearisome is such a wonderful thing for a child. Just look at the solemn faces of the little boys as they sit astride the brave wooden steed in the carousal! "Sonny, don't you like it? Why aren't you laughing?" exclaims the astonished mother.

A child is still at that stage of development when motion seems something wonderful. Is it possible that in this a secret (unconscious) sex-motive, such as is often felt by one when being rocked or swung in a swinging boat, does not play a part? Many adults admit this well-known effect of riding. This is in all probability one of the most potent and most hidden roots of the passion for travelling. Freud very frankly asserts in his "Contributions to a sexual theory" that rhythmical motion gives rise to pleasurable sensations in children. "The jolting in a travelling wagon and subsequently in a railway train has such a fascination for older children that all children, at least all boys, sometimes in their life want to be conductors and drivers. They show a curious interest in everything connected with trains and make these the nucleus of an exquisite system of sexual symbolism."

Be this as it may. The fact is that all the little ones want to become drivers of some vehicle, that they can play driver, rider, chauffeur, car, train, etc., for hours at a time, that in the first years of their lives their fantasies are fixed only on objects possessing the power of motion, beginning with the baby-carriage and ending with the aeroplane.

This stage lasts a variable period in different children. In some cases up to puberty and some even beyond this. I know boys who have almost attained to manhood who are still inordinately interested in automobiles and railways. In these cases we are dealing with a fixation of an infantile wish which will exercise a decisive influence on the individual's whole life. In most cases the first ideal loses its glamour before the magic of a uniform. The first uniform that a child sees daily is that of the "letter-carrier." In his favour, too, is the fact that he is always on the go, going from house to house. The "policeman" too, promenading up and down in his uniform, engages the child's fantasy. So too the dashing "fireman." Needless to say all these are very soon displaced and wholly forgotten in favour of the "soldier."

The love to be a soldier has its origin in many sources. Almost all boys pass through a period when they want to be soldiers. The wish to be a soldier is a compromise for various suppressed wishes. A soldier has been known to become a general and even a king. That fact is narrated in fairy tales, chronicled in sagas and recorded in history. One can manifest one's patriotism. Then there is the beautiful coloured uniform that the girls so love—and one is always going somewhere. For one is never just an ordinary soldier but a bold, dashing trooper, and—this above all!—one has a big powerful sword. Under the influence of these childish desires children plead to go to the military schools and the parents give their consent in the belief that it is the children's natural bent that speaks. Why, I tried to take this step when I was fifteen years old but—heaven be praised for it—was found physically unfit. My more fortunate friends who were accepted have for the most part subsequently discovered that they had erred in their youth.

The same thing happens with respect to the

other wishes of children, whether they become engineers, teachers, physicians, or ministers. The voice of the heart is deceptive and rarely betrays the individual's true gift. The biographies of great men may now and then give indications of talent manifested in childhood. But the contrary is also easily to be found. Very often hidden desires are concealed or masked behind one's choice of a calling. I know a man who became a physician because he longed to go far away, to go to the metropolis. In youth he had to be driven to practice his music—and yet music was his great talent and he should have become a musician.

What our children want to become . . . seldom denotes that they have a natural aptitude for a particular calling. They are to be regarded only as distorted symbols behind which the almost utterly insoluble puzzles of the childhood soul are concealed. When we are mature enough to know what we really want to become it is usually too late. Then we are children no longer. But then we would love to be children again and shed a furtive tear for the beautiful childhood that's dead . . . If we could be children again we'd know what we would like to be. No illusory wish would then tempt us from the right path, luring us like a will o' the wisp into the morass of destruction.

And this wish too is fulfilled. We become children again if we live long enough. But then, alas! our wishes have ceased to bloom.

Over the stubble-field of withered hopes we totter to our inevitable destiny. Everything seems futile, for all paths lead to one goal. Then we know what children would like to become, what they must become.

INDEPENDENCE

A pale, dark-complexioned young man, elegantly attired, sits before me. His hair is neatly parted on the side and boldly thrown back over his forehead ; he is clearly half snob and half artist ; in short, one of that remarkable type of young man that is so common in a modern metropolis. His complaints are the customary complaints of the modern neurotic. He is tired and weak, incapable of prolonged mental application. He is a clerk in an office, and has already lost one position because of his inability to use his brains any longer. With some difficulty his father had secured a position for him in a bank where a bright future seems to await him but where a dull present bears him down. All day it's nothing but figures, figures, figures. He cannot endure that. His patience is almost exhausted ; the figures swim before his eyes, and he makes more mistakes than is tolerable in an official of a bank. He begs me for a certificate that will officially vouch for his unendurable condition and make it possible for him to resign from his office in an honourable way before he is discharged for incompetence.

" Yes, and what will you do then ? Have you another position in prospect ? "

"Certainly," he replied, with a certain alacrity which was in striking contrast with his careless melancholy. "I want to make myself independent. I am not fitted for office work, and I can't bear to be bossed around and instructed by every Tom, Dick, or Harry who happens to have been on the job a few years longer than I."

"Ah! now I understand your inability to figure. You are living in a state of permanent psychic conflict. Because you have no desire to work you cannot work. But what kind of business do you wish to go into? What have you learned?"

"Learned? To tell the truth, only what one learns in a trade school. I don't want to go into business. I only want the certificate to show my father that my health will not permit me to work in an office. Do you think it's good for anybody to work from 9 a.m. to 6 p.m., with only one hour for luncheon?"

"That would be only eight hours work a day! I assure you that there are thousands who would be happy to work only so little. Shall you work less when you are independent?"

"Certainly. Then I won't have to work at all."

"So!" I replied in amazement. "I am curious to know what sort of business that is where one doesn't have to work. What do you intend to do when your father gives you money?"

A blissful smile passed over the interesting

youth's face like a beam of celestial light. "I know all about sports. I'm going to play the races!"

I must admit I was considerably taken aback. I know how reluctant to work many a modern man is whose whole energy is expended in dreams. But that a sensible man should think of such a thing was new to me. Such a peculiar motivation for the purpose of becoming independent. The matter kept running through my head a long time. I soon noticed that this youth was only an extreme type of a very common species —a species that expresses itself in a passion for independence. When we investigate the deeper causes of this passion we invariably find the desire to secure for oneself the utmost amount of pleasure from a very small investment. But independence is only apparently the coveted ideal; behind it lies not only the desire for freedom, not only the proud feeling of self-reliance. No, in many cases the kernel of the matter is—laziness.

Independence! Proud, brazen word! How many sacrifices hast thou not demanded and dost still demand daily! Who is ignorant of these little daily tragedies of which no newspaper makes mention! The salesman who, after he had for years enjoyed a care-free and assured position, has fallen a victim to the craving for independence, and has to contend with cares and worries so long that at last, broken down and battered, he renounces his beautiful dream and willingly submits his once proud neck to the yoke; the writer who starts his own newspaper and sees his hard-saved gold flow away in beautifully printed sheets; the actor who becomes the director of his own company; the merchant who builds his own factory,—an endless procession of men who wished to make themselves independent.

It would be one-sided not to admit that in addition to the aforementioned element of wanting to make one's work easier there is also a certain ambition to get ahead of one's neighbours. Modern man is linked to life by a thousand bonds. He is only a little screw in a vast machine —a screw that has little or no influence on the working efficacy of the complicated apparatus, that can be lightly thrown aside or replaced. We all feel the burden of modern life, and instinctively we all fret under it and work against it. We long to sever the link that ties us to commonplace day and to become the lever that sets the machinery in motion.

Stupid beginning! Hopeless and thankless! Who can be independent and absolute nowadays? Is there any calling that can boast of standing outside life? It is a delusive dream which beckons and betrays us. We change masters only. That's very simple. But we are far from becoming independent thereby. We have a hundred masters instead of one. The employee who has made himself "independent" has lost his master but becomes the slave of innumerable new tyrants to whose wills he must bow: his customers. Therein he resembles the so-called free professions which are in reality not free. The physician is dependent upon the whims of his patients; the lawyer woos the favour of his clients; the writer groans under the knout of the cruelest of all tyrants: the public. And, strange to say, it is this last calling that appeals to most persons as the ideal of independence. It is almost a weekly occurrence to see some discontented youngster or an unhappy girl with a thick manuscript in his or her portfolio, begging to be recommended to some publisher and thus open a writer's career to them. They want to become self reliant, independent. It is vain to point out to them that an author's bread is not sweetened with the raisins of independence. Others who have never written a line suddenly make up their minds to become journalists. They think that the will to become a journalist is all that is needed to be so. Evidences of adequate preparation and qualification they find in the excellence of their school compositions. They do not suspect that the journalist's independence is a myth that is credited only by those who have never smelled to journalism. That the journalist is the slave not only of the public but also of the hour. That not a minute of the day is his, and that he would gladly exchange his pen for any other, more massy tool, if such a thing were possible.

Dissatisfaction with one's calling is also one

of the factors that sets the feeling for independence in motion. Who is nowadays satisfied with his calling, or with himself ? ! This may be easily proved by referring to a striking phenomenon. In doing so we need not sing the praises of the " good old days." But happiness in one's work and contentment with one's calling were certainly much more common than they are now. Otherwise it could never have come to pass that the father's calling should be transmitted to the sons generation after generation. How is it with us to-day ? The physician cries : My son may be anything but a physician. The public official : My son shall be more fortunate than I ; under no circumstances shall he be a public official. The actor : Be what you will, my son, but not an artist ; art is the bitterest bread. The merchant wants to make a lawyer of his son, the lawyer a merchant, etc.

We envy others because we are all dissatisfied with ourselves and unhappy. The great ideal that floats before our eyes is to become a clipper of coupons. Money alone guarantees the road to independence. But if we were to ask the rich about this we would hear some surprising things. I know a lady who possesses a vast fortune and who is the absolute slave of her money. I recommended her to take a trip for her health's sake. She replied : " Do you think that I can go away for a week ? You have no idea of all the work I have to do. Now it's something with the bureau of taxes, now it's engaging a new superintendent! Then there are the receptions! I am busy from morning till night." When I advised her to hire a manager she laughed merrily: "I'd be in a fine fix if I did that! Then I would lose the only recompense I have: my independence!"

Wherever we look, the higher we go, the less of true independence do we find. What does the psychology of modern social feelings teach us? It shows us everywhere the same cry for independence which in the single individual we have described as the basic feeling of his social attitude. Norway wanted its independence and got it. Hungary stormily clamoured for independence. Ireland, Poland, Persia, India, Egypt, and numerous colonies are struggling for independence. In the structure of the State the urge for independence begets continual turmoil. Austria can sing a plaintive song as to this. The demand of certain states for autonomy is the outcome of the same motive.

Political tune—scurvy tune. However—wholly unintentionally our analysis brings us from the consideration of the individual to that of the group. That a modern state can never again attain that measure of independence that it once enjoyed is as clear to the political economist as to the sociologist. What we have said of the individual applies also to peoples.

Must we then conclude that there is no independence? Isn't it possible then for man to elevate himself above his environment and take a loftier point of view?

There certainly is such a thing as independence. But we must draw a sharp line of distinction between two different kinds of independence. There is an inner and an outer independence. But it is only the inner independence that one can hope to attain wholly. It alone is capable of giving us that modicum of outward independence which may be laboriously wrested from life. A healthy philosophy of life that frees the spirit, makes renunciation easier and wishing harder, and a certain spiritual and bodily freedom from wanting for things,—these alone can give us that independence that the world affords. That is why the poorest of the poor is more independent than the richest of the rich.

We all know the beautiful story of the king whose physicians promised him health if he could wear the shirt of a happy man. Mesengers searched every corner of the world but, alas! could not find a happy man, till finally they came upon a merry hermit in the thickest part of a dark forest who seemed to be perfectly happy. But he, the only happy man in the wide world, had no shirt!

We would have to divest ourselves of many shirts to become independent within. We wear and lug about with us numberless suits, wrappings, which cover up our true selves and apparently safeguard us, whereas in reality they drag us down to the base earth.

JEALOUSY

Has any one counted the victims of jealousy? Daily a revolver cracks somewhere or other because of jealousy; daily a knife finds entrance into a warm body; daily some unhappy ones, racked by jealousy and life-weary, sink into fathomless depths. What are all the hideous battles narrated by history when compared with the endless slaughters caused by this frightful passion! It enslaves man as no other passion does; degrades him, humiliates him, and makes him taste the hell of many other passions, such as envy, mistrust, revengefulness, fear, hate, anger, and poisons the meagre pleasure-cup that imparts a touch of sweetness to bitter life.

What is jealousy? Whence flow its tributaries? Is this the Danaidean gift to humanity? Is it the twin sister of love? Do we acquire it or is it born with us? It is surely worth while to consider every one of these questions and to attempt to determine the nature of this unholy passion.

To understand jealousy we must go far, very far back into the history of man's origin. Yes, far beyond man, as far as the animal world! For certain animals, intelligent animals, show clearly evidences of jealousy. Pet dogs resent it if their masters pet another dog. They are even jealous if the master caresses human beings. There are dogs who begin to whine if their master plays with or fondles his children. Very much the same thing is told of cats. Who of us on reading Freiligrath's gruesome ballad, "The Lion's Bride," has not felt the terror of the beast's furious jealousy?

Our observation of animals has taught us one of the fundamental characteristics of jealousy. Animals know very definitely what is theirs. They have a fine perception for what is theirs. Most dogs snarl even at their masters if they attempt to take their food from them. Their jealousy is the mood in which they express their possession, the egoism of their share. They defend as their possession even the affection to which they think themselves solely entitled.

The emotional life of the young shows the same phenomenon. They too do not know the distinction between thine and mine. What they happen to have in their hands is theirs and will defend it with their weak powers and loud howls. Many psychologists, including Percy, Compayné, Sully, Anfosse, Schion, Ziegler, consider the child an unmitigated egoist. Even in its love it is out and out egoistic and therefore extremely jealous. Young children's jealousy may attain an incredible degree of intensity. A little two-year-old girl cried incessantly if her mother took the baby brother in her arms.

A little boy was so jealous of his younger sister that he used to pinch her leg at every opportunity; having been smartly punished for it on one occasion he spared the little girl thereafter, but became afflicted with a peculiar compulsion neurosis: he pinched the legs of adults. Such experiences are of profound significance. They give us a glimpse of the primitive times when man had no idea yet of altruism. The whole world was his as far as his power, his strength, went. Man's jealousy developed out of this primary ego-feeling, out of his right to sole possession. Before man could be civilised this tremendous barrier had to be overcome. The first community, the first social beings, were the first stages of altruism and civilization.

From this period emanate the subterranean sources from which jealousy is fed. We have probably all become more or less altruistic. But always in conflict with ourselves, in conflict with the beast, in conflict with the savage within us. Even to this day the whole world belongs to each one of us. Our desires extend our property to infinity. What would we not own? What do we not desire? The wealth of the rich, the honour of the distinguished, the triumphs of the artist, to say nothing of his sexual triumphs. The less we can fulfil these desires the more do we cling to what we have, or, somewhat more accurately, could have had. For jealousy does not concern only what one actually possesses. Women may be jealous of men they do not love and do not even possess. They simply begrudge the other woman her conquest. Don Juans know this very well. The best way of conquering a woman is still the old, old way: to make love to her friend. In this case wounded vanity plays a part, of course. But what is vanity but the over-estimation of the Me, the striking emphasis laid on one's own value? And thus we again come back to the root of all jealousy: the pleasure in one's own possession, in one's embellished egoism.

Jealousy need not always have a sexual motive. A woman may be jealous of her husband's friend because he has been more successful than her husband. Her husband is her possession. He ought to be the foremost, he ought to have achieved the others' successes, so that his fame should revert to her too. Pupils are jealous of one another even though not a trace of a sexual motive may be demonstrable. We may be jealous of another's horses, dogs, furniture, virtues, honours, friendships, responsibilities, etc. Behind it there always is our brutal egoism, the desire for another's possessions, or at least the fear of losing one's own possession.

Jealousy is generally regarded as a pre-eminently feminine quality. Erroneously so. It would be more nearly correct to say that the heroic side of jealousy is to be found only in men. It is not a matter merely of chance that we have no feminine counterpart to Othello, Herod and the Count in Hauptmann's "Griselda." Jealousy in women has received a social valuation from men; it always has a smack of the ridiculous, pathological, or unjustified. It is a subject for satire, and is more often a comedy motive than a tragic reproach. This is due to the fact that woman's love is monopolised by men, whereas a man's loyalty is demanded by most women but attained only by very few. A man's infidelity is not a dramatic reproach because it is a daily occurrence and wholly in accord with the lax conception of the majority. A woman's infidelity is an offence against the sacred mandates imposed by—men. And therefore the jealousy of a man—be the subject of the passion a fool, a fop, an old man, or some other laughable type destined for cuckoldry—is a struggle for just possession, a conflict which always has an heroic effect, whereas a woman's jealousy is always a dispute for the sole possession of a man, a right which is disputed by a great majority (namely, the men, and even some women).

But there are men and women who are not jealous even though they love intensely. And with this we hit upon a second and important root of jealousy. Only one who contemplates an act of disloyalty against the object of his jealousy, or who, as a result of doubts about his own erotic powers, thinks he cannot gratify that object can be jealous. Of course I am not now speaking of justified jealousy based on facts, but of baseless, unjustified jealousy. Whence comes the suspicion that attributes infidelity to the beloved being? What is the driving power in these cases? Only the knowledge of one's true nature. Only they can be jealous, jealous without cause, who cannot guarantee for themselves. In other words: jealousy is the projection of one's own shortcomings upon the beloved.

If we find a woman who is all her life torturing her husband with her jealousy, complaining now that he has been looking at some woman too long, now that he stayed out too long, now that he was too friendly with one of her friends, etc., then it is the woman who has seen the weakness of her own character and who, in thought, is guilty of every infidelity which she will not admit even to herself. And in the same way faithless husbands who love their wives make the most jealous husbands. That is the vermuth potion which leaves with them a bitter after-taste as soon as they have made another conquest. Their own experiences entitle them to be jealous. Bachelors who had been philanderers and can boast of many conquests usually marry plain or unattractive women—alleging, by way of explanation, that they want to have the woman for themselves and not for others, meanwhile forgetting how often they themselves had been caught in the nets of homely women. For almost any woman who will permit herself to do so can find admirers, and ugliness is no protection against dramatic or comic marital infidelities.

The absence of jealousy in cases of intense affection usually, but not always, indicates a nature immune against all assaults. But those who are free from this passion need not therefore be puffed up. We are poor sinners all, and the time may come sooner or later for any of us in which we shall transfer our weaknesses upon others and become jealous. But it also happens that freedom from jealousy is a sign not of security but of stupidity, unlimited vanity. The woman is regarded as a paragon of all the virtues, without a touch of frailty. The husband may be an ideal specimen of an otherwise frivolous species. In these cases one's inadequacy is so covered up by our over-estimation of our endowments that comparisons are never instituted and projection is impossible.

Consequently baseless jealousy and baseless confidence will always be. And therefore we shall not follow Bleuler in his estimation of jealousy as one of the "unconscious commonplaces" which makes love valueless as "the plant-louse does the rose-bud." We shall recognise in it, when it is baseless, a disease of the soul occurring in persons whose cravings and realities do not coincide and who have with a heavy heart been forced to the recognition after cruel inner conflicts that their virtue is only an over-emphatic opposition to their weakness. Their jealousy has taken on a pathological (neurotic) character because of this repression and this relegating of their own desires into the unconscious. That is why all the logic of realities is effectless when opposed to the logic of the unconscious. One might almost say that jealousy is a cultural disease which results from the restrictions on our love-life imposed by law and morality. If so-called "free love" ever becomes a fact there will be far fewer cases of jealousy than we have to-day. That sounds plausible. But will life be more worth living when there will be no more jealousy? We gladly put up with jealousy if only our costly treasure of love continues secure. Would a life free from all jealousy and pain, a life without passions, be worth while? Is it not a fact that our possessions are most highly valued by us at the moment when we fear to lose them? . . . The sweetest harmonies are to be found only in contrasts. The wagon of life rolls with greater tempo over the endless lonely roads when it is harnessed to the passions.

CHILDHOOD FRIENDSHIP

An indescribably sweet breeze blows over the friendships of childhood. They are tender, delicate, pale blue petals that tremble with each stir of the childish soul and whose roots even then already penetrate down to the deep layers in which inherited instincts and tempting desires fertilise the soil of the passions. Its first friendship is a revelation for the child. Till then it loved its parents, its surroundings, its teacher. But behind this love the educational tendency was always in evidence. " You must love your parents because they are so good to you. You must respect your teacher because from him you get the knowledge that is indispensable to you in your life." Thus we make that love a duty for the child which ought, on the contrary, to make it conscious of its duties.

How different it all is in the case of friendship. Here the child can follow its natural inclinations. Here it can choose according to its own standards without having to listen to the dictates of its educators. And indeed one has thousands of opportunities to observe that a child is much more cautious than adults in the selection of its friends, that it will not accept a friend assigned it by its parents unless he meets with its approval, unless an unconscious urge pleads in his behalf.

How peculiar children are in their choice of a friend! Either he is the nicest or the finest, the quietest or the noisiest, the best or the worst, the strongest or the weakest. They prefer one whose traits are clearly and sharply defined, rather than one who is neither one thing nor the other. There must be something about the friend that they can admire; he must excel them in something. But it is not a bar to friendship that they excel the other in something.

Let no one say that it is an easy matter to read the souls of children! That their emotions are simple, that their soul's an open book! We can discover all the puzzling roots of love, even in the friendships of children, *e.g.*, sympathy, cruelty, desire, humility, and subjection.

It is my belief that we adults cannot love with the love we were capable of in childhood. We cannot hate so, cannot be so resentful, and cannot be so self-sacrificing. Alas! even our emotions become pallid with the years and can make a show of colour only with the aid of memory.

Let us watch a child that has entered into a close friendship. Is it not playing the same game that we adults later on designate as love? Have we forgotten the feverish impatience with which we awaited the hour of the friend's coming and how jealous we were if he stopped to converse with another? How we hated him then and how terribly unhappy we were? How we would have loved to cry aloud, if we had not been ashamed to betray such weakness. Have we forgotten how the hours flew when we were playing together, how we whispered dreadful and mysterious things to each other in the twilight, how passionately we embraced each other, and kissed, and how ready we were to give up our little treasures to our friends? There is but one time that resembles this friendship :—the time when a happy love makes a wooer a sweet child again.

Even in a child's soul the hunger for love cries aloud and will not be stilled. For a love that is more than a love of parents, for a love that is touched with that dark power which at a later period shapes the life of man to its will.

Oh! blessed time, in which our yearning for a second human being is so easily gratified! Blessed time, in which we do not yet feel the hot breath of burning desires when the arm of a beloved being entwines us, in which the threatening fist of Destiny does not pin us to the ground at the moment when we think we are plucking down the sky! The mirror of our soul still reflects pure innocence; we do not yet suspect that the passions that set the waters in motion must also stir up the muddy ooze that lies at the bottom.

Childhood friendship is the school of love. Without such friendship the child is impoverished and forever loses the power to love. Look at the mothers' darlings whose mothers took the place of friends! See how they are bound to their mothers by all their emotions, by all the bonds of their souls, incapable of breaking loose from the love for the mother and founding another generation. The stupidest dream of parents is the wish to be the friends of their children. But are we not deceiving ourselves? Is such a thing possible? Is there not between ourselves and our children a world of disappointments and buried hopes? Are there not here yawning chasms in whose depths wild torrents carry away the residue of past years, chasms which cannot be bridged? Say what we will, only a child can be a child's friend!

And there is much food for reflection in this. The child is surrounded by so much authority, so much school, so much dignity, so much law, that it would have to break down under the weight of all these restraints if it were not saved from such a fate by meeting with a friend. In secret conferences, at first in whispers and only in hints, but subsequently more and more clearly and distinctly, the road to life is outlined. The gods are dethroned, or, at any rate, are not feared so much; little jokes about the teacher are the beginning, and gradually the excess of parental authority goes tumbling till it assumes just proportions. The way to freedom of thought, the way to independence, the way to individuality is opened. What the child could not have accomplished alone was a mere toy with the help of another. And the friendship grows ever prouder and more intimate the more the child loses the feelings enforced upon it.

One great mystery, the child's eternal question, occupies its mind more than most parents, most persons, will believe: the question about the origin of man, the question which is customarily answered with a childish tale about a stork (or a big tree in heaven, a large cabbage, or a department store), a tale with which the clever little ones make fools of their elders who go on repeating for many years a story they had long ago ceased to believe. Behind all the child's curiosity there lurks the one great question: "Where do children come from?" One will never go wrong in concluding that a child who is plaguing his elders with a thousand stupid and clever questions is suffering from a kind of obsession, an obsessive questioning, behind which lies the one great and important question that troubles all children. On this subject the child cannot speak with its parents. Instinctively it feels that here is a great mystery that is being withheld from it and whose solution the parents have put off for a future time. It is during childhood friendship and in connection with this question that sexuality plays its first trump. It is a pity that human beings so easily forget their own childhood, else parents would not be so blind in this regard. In the northern psychologist's, Arne Gaborg's, best work "By Mama" there is a wonderful scene copied direct from nature: Two little girls are sitting on the basement stairs whispering to each other their latest bit of information about the great mystery; gradually it grows dark and an inexplicable dread of something great, threatening, mysterious, fills their trembling souls; it is that fear which faithfully accompanies love throughout life and whose dark wing has just barely brushed their innocent childhood.

The child gets older and friendship changes its nature. Life and its claims interpose their authority. Into the quiet and unselfish friendship of childhood, into the pure and simple childish harmonies there penetrate various over- and under-tones whose inharmonious character is not discovered until long after. Envy, egoism, covetousness, cunning, distrust,—all these feelings steal their way into the childhood friendship, and finally friendship degenerates into what Moebius has so aptly named *Phantom-practice*. Young obstetricians train their unskilled hands on "phantoms" (or mannikins) to fit them for the serious requirements of their art. Something exactly like this is the conduct of young adolescents, especially girls, who are still half-child and already half-woman. To a girl the admiration of a girl friend takes the place of a lover's wooing; to be kissed by her results in a dream of being kissed by a man. Recently biology has developed the idea, erroneously attributed to Otto Weininger, that every human being is a mixture of both sexes. Before puberty the two elements *M*. and *F*., male and female, must balance. The child is bisexually constituted, and therefore every friendship is in a certain sense a love affair. About the time of sexual maturity the sexuality of every individual triumphantly asserts itself. This is the great moment when childhood friendship has fulfilled its mission. It is as if the child were now freeing itself from the yoke of its own sex and entering the arena equipped for the battle of love.

This also explains why childhood friendships so seldom are preserved and carried over into adult life. The friendships of adults are based upon different foundations. Now it is the thinking, reflecting, conscious being who seeks a fellow combatant who he hopes will fully understand (and sympathise with) him. Higher interests determine their friendships. But it is no longer so deeply rooted as childhood friendship. It no longer requires the co-operation of the instinctive emotions.

Now and then one comes across persons who are always children, whom not even the bitterest experiences can strip of the pollen linked with their emotions. They are the only ones capable of true friendship even in their old age. They spread friendship with the sweet smile of the child; they do not love for the sake of the advantages to be derived; they do not even ask whether they are their friends' friend. Ah! If we could be such a child again! Or if we could but find it!

EATING

I was once invited to the house of a certain writer who had made a name for himself by several very clever novels and had acquired a fortune by the publication of a successful journal. He was now living on an estate in the country, retired from active life, spending his days in luxurious peace. Much too soon, as I very quickly found out. For he was in no sense old. A man about fifty whose eyes still looked challengingly at the world. His look had in it nothing of the asceticism of one who is tired of life. No; here the fire of secret passions still blazed; here one could still detect power, ambition, and desires.

Much in his conduct seemed puzzling to me. A stony calm, a certain lassitude in his movements,—an enforced pose calculated to conceal the internal restlessness which his eyes could not help betraying.

Only when the time to eat came he became all life. Then he stretched his neck aloft, that he might see clearly the dish that was being brought in. His nostrils dilated as if the sooner to inhale the delightful aroma. His mouth made remarkable twitching movements and his tongue moved over his thin lips with that peculiar rapid movement that one may observe in a woman when she is engaged in animated conversation with a man. He became restless, fidgetted nervously in his chair, and followed tensely the distribution of the food by his wife, a corpulent, energetic and almost masculine woman, who, very naturally and to his secret distress, helped her guests first. Finally—much too late to suit him—he received his portion. First he regarded his food with the eye of an expert, turning it from side to side with his knife and fork. Then he cut off a small piece and rolled it about in his mouth with audible clucking and smacking of his tongue, let it rest on his tongue awhile, his face the meantime assuming an expression of visionary ecstasy. It was easy to see that for him eating had become the day's most important task. During the meal he never stopped talking of the excellence of the food, all the while smacking his tongue and lips, and literally expounding a system of culinary criticism.

When finally, to my great relief, the grace after dinner had been pronounced, I hoped at last to be done with the wearying, unpleasant chatter about eating. But this time I had really reckoned without my host.

"What shall we serve our guests to-morrow, my dear?" the gourmand inquired of his sterner half.

"To-morrow? The big white goose with the black patch."

"The big white goose with the black patch! Ah! She'll taste wonderful! You don't know how childishly happy it makes me. Come, let me show you the white goose with the black patch!"

Resistance was useless. I had to go into the poultry-yard, where my host stopped in front of a well-fed goose. "She'll make a fine roast! I am greatly pleased with this goose."

No matter what subject was discussed, political, literary, or economic, the main motif kept recurring: "I love to think of the big white goose with the black patch!"

The meaning of gourmandism then suddenly flashed on me. What passions must this man have suppressed, how much must he have renounced, before his craving for pleasure had found new delights in this roundabout way! Behind this monomaniac delight in eating, thought I, there must lurk a great secret.

And such was indeed the case. My amiable host was really his wife's prisoner. While he was residing in the capital he had begun to indulge in a perversion. His vice grew on him to such an extent that it threatened to destroy everything, health, fortune, mind, ambition, personality, spirit, everything. There was nothing left for him to do but to tell his wife all and implore her assistance in saving him. The virile woman soon hit on the only remedy. He became her prisoner. They broke off all relationships that bound them to their social group. Most of the year they spent in the country and lived in the city only two or three winter months. The time was spent in eating and card playing, to which fully half of the day was devoted. He was never alone. At most he was permitted to take a short walk in the country. His wife had charge of the family treasury, with which he had nothing to do. Of course, this did not cure his pathological craving, but it made gratification impossible. And gradually there began to develop in him the pleasure for delicate dishes. In this indirect way he satisfied a part of his sensuous craving. Thus he transformed his passion. His meals took the place of the hours spent in the embraces of a lover. For him eating was a re-coinage of his sexuality.

Is this an exceptional case, or is this phenomenon the rule ? This is the first question that forces itself on our attention. An answer to it would take us into the deeps of the whole sexual problem. But let us limit ourselves for the present only to what is essential for an answer to our immediate question. Between hunger and love there is an endless number of associations. The most important is this : both are opposed by one counter-impulse, namely, disgust. Both love and hunger are desires to touch, (to incorporate or to be incorporated with the desired object) ; disgust is the fear of doing so. Love is accompanied with a counter-impulse, a restraining influence, which we call shame. But this very feeling, shame, is manifested by certain primitive peoples in connection with eating. In Tahiti, says Cook, not even the members of the family eat together, but eat seated several metres apart and with their backs to one another. The Warua, an African tribe, conceal their faces with a cloth while they are drinking. The Bakairi are innocent of any sense of shame in connection with nakedness, but never eat together.

The Viennese psychiatrist Freud, the Englishman Havelock Ellis (" The Sexual Impulse "), and the Spanish Sociologist Solila, regard the sucking of the breast by an infant as a kind of sexual act which creates permanent associations between hunger and love. And the language we speak has coined certain turns of expression which bring these connections out unmistakably and which have great interest for us as fossilisations of primitive thought processes and as rudiments of cannibalism. Note, for example, the following expressions : " I could bite her " ; or, " I love the child so I could eat it up ! " But we express even disgust, aversion and hatred in terms of eating, *e.g.*, " I can't stomach the fellow," or, " he turns my stomach," " she is not to my taste," etc.

On the other hand the names of certain dishes reveal connections with other emotional complexes than the pure pleasure of eating. There is an everyday symbolism which we all pass by blindly. Let him who has any interest in this subject read Rudolph Kleinpaul's book, "Sprache ohne Worte" (Language without Words). This symbolism plays a much more important rôle than we are wont to admit. For it alone is capable of interpreting the puzzling names of the various delicacies on the bill of fare. We are cannibals, for we eat "Moors in their 'Jackets'" (a fine revenge on the tawny cannibals!) "poor knights," "master of the chase," "apprentice-locksmith," and many more of the same kind. "Bridal roast" holds an important place in the menus of the whole world. Social inferiority is compensated for by numerous royal dishes . . . *e.g.*, steak-a-la-king, cutlet-a-la-king, chicken-a-la-king, royal pudding, etc., etc. One who will take the trouble, as Kleinpaul did in his "Gastronomic Fairy-tale," to follow up these things, will discover many remarkable links with unconscious ideas. We are really hemmed in on every side by fairy tales. Every word we speak, every name we utter, has its story. And the many fairy tales in which children are devoured by wolves, witches, man-eaters, and sea-monsters, together with the tales in which so much is said about man-eating cannibals, reveal to us a fragment of our pre-historic past in which love and hate actually resulted in persons being eaten. In their naïveté our children betray this very clearly. When the little ones eat maccaroni, noodles, or similar dishes, they often make believe they are eating up somebody.

But, " something too much of this." Let us turn our attention again to the epicures, the little progeny of a great race. It is not difficult to divide them into five classes according to which one of the five senses is being chiefly gratified during the eating process. First, there are the " Voyeurs," to use the term so aptly coined by the French with reference to a phenomenon in the sexual sphere. They must " see " before they can enjoy. To see is the important thing with them. The dishes must be served neatly and must look inviting. They are the admirers of the many-coloured adornments on patisserie, of torts, cakes, and puddings built in the shape of houses, churches, towers, animals, wedding-bells, etc. They reckon their pleasures by the colour nuances of their foods. Their chief delight is in the fore-pleasure derived through the eyes. (This is clearly implied in the popular phrase " a feast for the eyes.")

Not quite as common are the listeners " who are thrown into a mild ecstasy by the sizzling of a roast, the cracking of dry crumbs, and the fiz of certain liquids." Numberless are the " smellers " whose sensitive noses drink in the aroma of the foods as their chief delight, whereas the eating, as such, is performed mechanically, as an unavoidable adjunct. Such persons can revel in the memories of a luscious dish, and many of their associations are linked with the olfactory organ. The pleasure in offensive odours, such as arise from certain cheeses, garlic, rarebits, and wild game is to some extent a perversion nutritional instinct and betrays innate relationships to sexual aberrations, as are unequivocally indicated by certain popular ditties and college songs. The folk-lore of all nations teems with hints at such things.

An important group, the fourth, is that of the "toucher." As we know the tongue of man is the most important of the gustatory organs, even though it has not that primacy and importance which it has in many animals. Such "touchers" derive their greatest pleasure from the mere touching of the food with the tongue. They prefer smooth and slippery foods, *e.g.*, oysters which they can suck down, and they love to roll the food around in their mouths. It goes without saying that these persons are also "tasters," as indeed the majority of eaters are. But for all that, these have their own peculiar traits; whereas the feeling of fullness or satiety is to many persons a kind of discomfort, and a full stomach gives rise to a disagreeably painful sensation, to these "touchers" a full stomach means the most delightful sensation the day has to offer.

Of the "gourmands" (literally "the relishers") we need not say much. The whole world knows them; to describe them many words and phrases have been coined, *e.g.* sweet-toothed, cat-toothed, epicures, etc.

As might have been expected, these various

forms are often combined in one person, and your genuine gourmand eats with all his senses. We need only keep our eyes open at a restaurant to observe that most persons show some trace of epicurism. Very few resist the temptation to follow the platter the waiter is carrying to some table. (Almost every one likes to see what his neighbour is eating.) We may be discussing art, politics, love, or what not, yet watch carefully how much the person serving is taking for himself or dishing out for the others, and how little he is leaving for us. Most of the time in these cases we are the victims of an optical deception. Our neighbour's portion always seems bigger than ours. Hunger and envy magnify the other person's portion and minimise ours. And is it not an every-day experience that we order what our neighbour is eating? "Waiter, what is that you served the man over there? Bring me the same!"

How a person eats always reveals something of his hidden personality. In the case of most human beings at meals the same thing happens that one may observe at the menagerie during feeding-time: the peacefully reposing lion becomes a beast of prey. That is why beautiful women become ugly when they eat and lose their charm, cease to become interesting when they are seen eating. It is not a meaningless custom that we honour distinguished persons by dining them. By so doing we create a situation in which there is no superiority and in which we feel ourselves at one with the great man and on a level with him.

Much more complicated than the psychology of the ordinary eater is that of the gourmand, who always seems even to himself to be an exceptional kind of person and who has in unsuspected ways enlarged the sphere of possible pleasures. In most of these cases we shall find that they are persons of whom life has demanded many renunciations. Just as the habitual drinker rarely stupifies himself because of the pleasure he takes in drinking but mostly out of a desire to drown in unconsciousness a great pain, to draw the veil over some humiliation, disillusionment, failure, or disappointment, so the gourmand likewise compensates himself for his lost world. He has the same right to the pleasures of life that others have. Well for him that he is capable of securing his portion in this way!

Inexperienced humanitarians long for the time when eating will be superfluous, when a few pills of concentrated albumin combined with a few drops of some essential ferment will supply the necessary energy for our mental and physical labours. What a stupid dream! If such a time ever came, how unhappy humanity would be! The most of mankind, truth compels me to say, live only to eat. For them "eating" is synonymous with "life." With the discovery of such pills the wine of life would be drawn. No! No! No! If there were no such thing as eating we should have to invent it to save man from despairing. Eating enables one who has suffered shipwreck on Life's voyage to withdraw into a sphere which once meant the greatest happiness to all human beings and still means it to all animals. One takes refuge in the primal instincts where one is safe and comfortable, until Mother Earth again devours and assimilates him before she awakes him to new life. We are all eternal links in an unending chain of links.

And that is the whole meaning of eating: life and death. Every bite we eat means a quick death for myriads of living things. They must die that we may live. And so we live by death until our death gives life to others.

It's no mere accident that Don Juan is summoned from the feast to his death.

ARE WE ALL MEGALOMANIACS?

There is no sharp dividing line between health and disease. One shades off into the other by imperceptible gradations. Disease grows out of health organically. There are a thousand transitions from the one to the other; a thousand fine threads link them together, and often not even the best physicians can determine where health ceases and disease begins. As Feuchtersleben says, there is no lyric leap in the epic of life. Nor do delusions make their entry unheralded into a well ordered mental life. Delusions slumber in all of us and wait for their prey. The quiet normal being is just as subject to them as the raving maniac with rolling congested eyes. We need only open our eyes understandingly upon the bustle and tumult of life to be able to exclaim with Hans Sachs: "Madness! Everywhere madness!"

Every form of insanity, one may say, has a physiological prototype. Melancholia takes for its model the little depressive attacks of everyday life; mania has its prototype in the unrestrained enthusiasm of the baseball "fan"; and even the various forms of paranoia, the true insanity, have their typical representatives among normal persons. To bring out this kinship we need no better example than that offered by the delusion of greatness. This delusion is so bound up with the requirements of the human psyche, so organically knit together with the ego, that it constitutes an indispensable element of our ethical consciousness. Every one of us thinks himself the wisest, best, most conscientious, and so forth. Each one thinks himself indispensable. It is this delusional greatness of the normal person which makes life tolerable under even the hardest conditions. It gives us the strength to bear all our humiliations, disappointments, failures, and the "whips and scorns of time."

Of course we are very careful to conceal this delusional greatness from the rest of the world. We all have our secret chapels in which we offer daily prayers and into which no one, not even our nearest, is permitted even to glance. In this chapel our idol sits enthroned, the prototype of majesty, "our ego," before whom we bend our knees in humble supplication. But out there—in the world without—it is different. There we play the role of the humble, respectful, subservient fellow. We swear allegiance to alien gods and mock our ego and its powers.

But sometimes the delusional greatness breaks out with pathological elementary force. We ought to keep our light under a bushel, trudge along with the multitude, day in, day out. Then all would be well. But destiny must not lift us to heights where our behaviour cannot escape observation and every one of our thoughts will be deduced from our actions. Success must not narcotise us to the extent of depriving us of that vestige of self-criticism which we so imperatively need in whatever situation life may place us. Success does not pacify the roaring of our megalomania. Success goads it with a thousand lashes of the whip so that it becomes restive and escapes from the security of the preserves of the soul. Is this still a healthy manifestation? Or are we already in the realm of the pathological? Is it the first delusion or the ultimate wisdom?

The delusion of greatness penetrates whole classes of humanity, infecting them like a subtle poison against which there is almost no immunity. We have only to refer to the "affairs" of all kinds of artists of the first, second, and third rank. The delusional greatness of the artist usually appears along with the belittling mania displayed by his confreres, his immediate competitors. The higher we esteem ourselves, the more we depreciate our fellow climbers. That is the reason why the artist, drunk with his own ego, loses the power to be just, to measure the work of others by any but an egocentric standard. Should any one venture to show this megalomania its true image in the calm mirror of justice, he would be characterized a malicious enemy. In the struggle to maintain the hypertrophied ego-consciousness the delusion of greatness is assisted by a willing servant: the delusion of persecution.

Along with the artist class there are many other vocations which to a certain extent gratify the delusion of greatness. In some callings this is a kind of idealistic compensation for the poor material returns. The megalomania of the Prussian officer, or the American professor (who are the butts of even the so-called harmless comic-journals) is an example. A close second to this is the megalomania of certain exclusive student organizations, patriotic megalomania, etc.

We can no longer escape a generalization. We note that delusional greatness is a compensation for some privation or hardship. This is especially illuminating with reference to that patriotic delusional greatness which has nothing whatever to do with a wholly justifiable self-consciousness. The self-consciousness of the Briton emanates from his proud history and the imposing power of his nation. But we note that it is especially small nations, who ought in reason to be very modest, who are guilty of a tremendous self-overestimation. And they do not scruple to invent an illustrious past which is calculated to lend some show of historic justification for the national delusion. *Exempla sunt odiosa.*

This mechanism teaches us how to estimate folk-psychology. A people behaves like an individual. So that our findings with reference to the psychology of individuals may be applied to whole races, and *vice versa.*

And here we note that the individual's delusional greatness invariably has one and the same root: it is an over-compensation for an oppressive diminution of the ego-consciousness. The daily life about us offers innumerable proofs of this assertion. Persons particularly prone to delusional greatness are those who suffer from certain defects and who in youth had been subjected to painful, derisive, scornful, or depreciative criticism. Amongst these we find especially the halt, the lame, the partly blind, the stutterer, the humpbacked, the red-haired, the sick, etc.—in short, persons with some stigma. By the mechanism of over-compensation such individuals may manifest inordinately ambitious natures. Is it accidental that so many celebrated generals—Cæsar, Napoleon, Prince Eugene, Radetzky—were of small stature ? Was it not precisely this smallness of stature which furnished the driving power that made them "great" ? Instead of looking for the essence of genius in peculiar bodily proportions (which Popper finds to be in a long trunk and short legs !) it would prove a more gratifying task to ferret out those primary factors that have brought about an unusual expenditure of psychic energy in one particular direction.

A very brilliant and suggestive hypothesis (advanced by Dr. Alfred Adler) attempts to account for all superior human gifts as an over-compensation for some original "inferiority." Even if this principle may not prove true in every case, it can be demonstrated to have played a part in the development of many a case of superior merit in some field of mental endeavour. We are all familiar with largely authentic anecdotes about distinguished scholars, who have just managed to squeeze through in their final professional examinations. In their case, too, by over-compensation a conviction of their inferiority brought about a heightened interest in their work and this interest then became permanently fixed.

Unawares we have wandered from the delusional greatness to true greatness. But who will presume to decide what is true greatness and what delusion? How many discoverers and inventors were ridiculed and their imposing greatness stigmatized as delusion, and how many intellectual ciphers rejoiced in the applause and the worship of their contemporaries! It is this fact which encourages a megalomaniac to permit the criticism of his contemporaries to "fly by him as the idle wind which he respects not." If it is not true that all greatness is ignored, the opposite is true: every ignored person is one of the great ones. At least he is so to himself. Delusional greatness unites both criticism and recognition in a single tremendous ego-complex.

The roots of this delusion, as of all purely

psychic maladies, are infantile. There was a time in the lives of all of us when we were the victims of a genuinely pathological delusion of greatness. In the days of our childhood we were consumed by a longing to be "big." At first it was only the desire to be a "big man," to be grown up. A little later and our desires fluttered across the sea of our thoughts like sea-gulls or flew like falcons into the unknown vast. We were kings, ministers of state, princes, ambassadors, generals, trapeze artists, conductors, firemen, or even butlers.

And yet we are all surprised when a butler plants himself squarely before the door and assumes the easy port of a person of some standing and identifies himself with the master of the house and graciously dispenses his domestic favours. Are we then, much better, more sensible, or freer from prejudice? We too stand before the doors of our desires and act as if we believed that they are realities which we are obliged to guard.

RUNNING AWAY FROM THE HOME

Once more the physician felt the young woman's pulse. " But it's impossible : you must not go out to-day ; you are running the risk of a relapse. You stay in your beautiful home that you have furnished so cosily, so comfortably, and with such good taste. I have no objection, however, to your inviting a few friends, having a little music, chatting, gossiping, but—stay home ! "

The pretty self-willed woman pursed her lips at this and though her grimace was very becoming to her it seemed a little to vex her old doctor who had known her from her infancy. Somewhat irritated, he continued :—

" I don't just know what you mean by the moue. Must I point out the dangers of exposing yourself to a ' fresh cold ' ? Do you insist on making a Sunday of every week-day ? First, it's a café, then, a restaurant ! From a hot room into the cold, moist, windy atmosphere of a winter night ! "

" But staying home is so stale and unprofitable," wailed the young woman. " Home ! I'm home all the live-long week ! Sunday, one wants a change ! I want to see human beings ! You are very disagreeable to day, Doctor ! "

The old doctor gently patted the young woman's cheek. "Still the same self-willed, obstinate child that will butt it's head against the wall. Ah, you seem to have forgotten how nice and sociable your parents' home was. Those never-to-be-forgotten Sundays! How we used to congregate there, a group of intimates —the young ones chatting and singing while the older ones played cards,—and every Sunday was a real holiday! And when things got a little more lively, then young and old romped together. Do you remember? Now and then someone would read us a new poem or the latest novel. How we did enjoy those Sundays! And how unforced and unconventional it all was! We would get our cup of tea or coffee and were as happy as happy as could be. But the things that are going on now seem to me, in my rôle as physician, to be a kind of neurosis, a something that I should call 'the flight from home!'"

"But, my dear doctor, must it be a neurosis? Is it necessary to brand everything as a disease?"

"But it is a disease and its character as such is very clearly established by this one element: its compulsive character. The flight from the home is a compulsive idea, that is, an idea against which logic, persuasion, and appeals are of no avail."

"I think you are going too far," replied the young woman. "If I insist upon going to the café to-day, I do it not because I do not like my home;

no, I do it because at the café I get a kind of stimulation which I do not get at home. There I can look through various journals and papers that I cannot afford to have at home. I get a chance to see friends and acquaintances whom I could not receive at home so often. And the main thing, at any rate for a young woman who still wishes to please—and that, I am sure you won't resent, you dear old psychologist!—the main thing is that there I see new people and—am seen by them. I know that in return I must put up with a few unpleasantnesses. Yes, there is the stuffy and smoky atmosphere, the continual din and noise, and so forth. But I really do think that we moderns need these things. We are not born to rest."

The physician shook his head.

"No! Never! You will pardon, I hope, my telling you that yours is a very superficial psychology and does not go down to the heart of the problem. To the modern civilized human being his home seems to be an extremely disagreeable place. All his life he is fleeing from his home, from his environment, and—yes!—even from himself. An inner restlessness, a discontent that cannot be quenched, a nervous stress permeates the people of our time. What they possess seems to them stale, worthless. What they pursued madly disappoints them when they have attained it. They crave for change because they do not know how to make the best use of the present and of their possessions.

How else can we understand the phenomenon that the whole world is happy to get away from the home and those who are incapable of running away long to do so? For, I am sure if you will give it careful thought you will confess that you call 'experience' only what happens to you away from home. The days at home don't count. Am I right?"

"Only partly so, my dear doctor. It does not tally with the facts—because nothing can be experienced at home. And I would be only too happy to receive my friends here daily, if it were possible. Don't you know that servants would rebel at it? That they want to have their day off? That I must not expect them to do such work as waiting on my guests every Sunday? Why even on week days the invitation of guests causes a little rebellion in the ordinary household!"

"And why must there be invitations? Must your visitors always be guests? Just look at Paris! There you may drop in on any of your acquaintances after 9 p.m. You may or you may not get a cup of tea. You chat a few hours and then depart. With us that's impossible, because our so-called "Teas" have assumed proportions which were formerly unknown. You invite one to come and have tea with you but instead of that you serve a luncheon and make a veritable banquet of it, going to a lot of trouble and expense, a course which must have bad consequences."

"Do you know, doctor, I think you are a magician! Its only conventional politeness that makes us receive our guests cordially. But you must serve your friends something when you invite them for a little chat, mustn't you?"

"There you are again! How beautifully you chatter away so superficially! No, my dear! Nowadays one no longer invites friends to spend a pleasant time with them, but to show them a new gown or to impress them with the new furnishings. The main thing is to poison the friend's peace of mind. If the guest's face betrays all the colours of envy then the hostess has attained the acme of delight. One might almost say that their dissatisfaction with their lot in life drives human beings on to stir up discontent in the hearts of others. This sowing of dragon's teeth bears evil fruit. For at the next 'tea' the friend has a more beautiful dress, perhaps some other new sensation, and her husband's achievements and income mount to supernatural heights, if one is to believe the hostess' eloquent speeches. Finally, there is no possibility of out-trumping her and there is nothing left to do but, in a more moderate tone, to fight out the rivalry on a neutral soil. The restaurant or the café is this neutral soil."

"And what are your objections to this neutral soil?"

"My objections? The people lose the greatest pleasure that they could derive from one another.

At home it must happen now and then that the walls which separate the inmates from one another fall, the wrappings that encase our inmost being burst, and soul speaks to soul. At home it is possible to devote the time to the nobler delights that life has to offer. At one time there can be—as there was in your own parents' home—a reading, on another occasion singing or music. And would it be such a terrible misfortune to spend one's holiday with one's family, to be one with them, reviewing the week that is past or playing with the children and being a child again? Don't you see that you are giving up the gold of home-life and pursuing the fool's-gold of pleasure outside the home? You do see it, you know I am right, and a little voice within you implores and pleads: 'Stay home! Stay home! here you are safe and comfortable!' But another power, a power that is stronger than you, drives you out, rushes you away from peace and quiet to restlessness, and whirls you about. And this whirl, you call 'life.' What have these empty pleasures to offer us? What inspiration for the work-a-day life do they leave behind? Is this anything less than just simply killing the hours? I don't want to spin out the old stuff about the dangers of pleasures, getting over-heated, catching cold, overtaxing one's nervous energies, losing one's sleep, etc. As to these things, I must admit, there is a great deal of exaggeration. One ought not to fly from pleasures. But they ought to serve as inspiring exceptions to break, as it were, the day, just as a trip does."

"But, my dear doctor, now you've caught yourself in your own springe. Is not a trip a flight from the home?"

The young woman laughed hilariously. But the doctor—now that he had assumed the rôle of preacher—did not permit himself to be put off or confused.

"Of course, the ordinary journey does belong to my theme. A trip may, in fact, constitute the crisis in our neurosis. A crisis that we must all go through, for we all—I am sorry to say, I too—suffer from this compulsive idea. As after every other crisis the invalid is for a time restored to health, so is it also after a trip. But only for a short time. A few weeks—and the compulsive idea is again manifest and the flight from the home begins again."

"Come, now, doctor!" interrupted the convalescent, "travelling is a necessity. As you so aptly said, we want to break the monotony of the day—to get out of the customary environment."

"That's just what I want to designate as the chief symptom of the neurosis of our time. Everyone wants to get away from the customary environments. Everybody makes attempts at flight. Whether they succeed depends upon other social factors. Why is the customary environment repugnant to you?"

"Because I crave a change. I do not know

why. But I have an instinctive longing for it."

"There you have it, my dear. It's just as I said: It's a compulsive idea. The flight from one's environment, from one's home, from one's furniture, is the same as the flight from one's house. To me every piece of furniture that I have used a long time has become so dear and so much a part of myself that I do not like to give them away and can only with difficulty part with them. And if I were to come into possession of a vast fortune to-day I could not renounce these dear associates to whom I am bound by so many memories. With all their shortcomings and modesty they are a thousand times dearer to me than the most beautiful English or secessionist furnishings. I'll confess that in these matters I am not at all modern. For the moderns are glad when they can change something, and so they change their furniture, their carpets, their pictures, etc. About every ten years there is a change in the fashions and your housewife cannot bear not to be in style. One day you enter her house and you find new rooms. And just as the furnishings in the house are changed from time to time, so the residence too must be changed frequently—in fact, everything that can be changed is changed: The servants, the family phsyician, the music teacher, and, where it is possible, the husband and even the wife."

The young woman reflected a little. "There is much truth in what you say. It is in fact a tremendous flight that we see enacted everywhere about us, a flight from oneself and from one's environment. If I were to judge by my own feelings I should say that this fleeing has its origin in our life's needs. We woman all have a large 'Nora' element in us and are waiting for the 'miracle.' Inasmuch as we cannot find it at home we look for it elsewhere. Believe me, doctor, most women do not fall because of sensual appetites. No! they fall because they crave for some experience. We experience too little. The monotony of the days asphyxiates us. And this great whirl of life, this senseless running after a change—as you call it—is only because our hearts are discontented, because our spirits are wrecked by the monotony and insipidity of our lives. Do you think that it will ever be different ?"

"Why not, pray ? Some day a great physician must arise, an apostle of human love, whose voice will pierce the whirl and who will be capable of opening man's stupid eyes : A new religion would do it, a religion that would satisfy all of humanity's longings, a religion of work and the joy of life. Our time is ripe for a Messiah. Whether he will come——."

"Ah, he has come," said the charming young woman, her face beaming. "For me you are the Messiah of domesticity ! You have cured me of my flight neurosis. I shall stay home to-day, and as often as I can do so."

The old doctor took his leave with animated

steps. With the power of his words he had once again reformed a human being.

But his joy was short-lived. That afternoon, as he walked by a café on the main thoroughfare his eyes fell on a vivacious group within. And there he saw his recalcitrant patient who had evidently gone out only to get a chance to discuss thoroughly with her friends the theme: "The flight from the house."

DEAD-HEADS

"Are there any people who still pay for tickets?" I was asked in all seriousness by a man, who, as a result of his numerous connections, had been able to develop the art of getting passes to its utmost possibilities.

Ridiculous though the question may sound to some, there is, nevertheless, something very profound in it. The pursuit after passes is in our day a favourite "sport" of residents of large cities. To most such people a journalist or a writer is not an artist who laboriously strives to give adequate expression to his thoughts, who has to listen to the secret voices within his breast and to translate them into the language of every day. No, in their mind a writer is the Croesus of passes. He only sits in front of his desk, as there accumulate before him green, blue, and red tickets, the magic keys that open the doors to all the temples of art without having to go to the trouble of digging into his money bag and experiencing the pleasure of paying out his shining coins. And they take it ill of the Croesus that he is so niggardly as to guard his treasures so greedily and not make everybody he comes in contact with happy by distributing the little papers. For to them getting a pass is considered a great piece of good fortune, almost like drawing a grand small prize in a lottery. It enables one to temporarily enjoy the greatest sensation in life: pleasure without cost. That is, it should so enable one.

With a pass one gets everything,—the respect of the upper classes, the right to be rude and the enforcement of courtesy. If it were possible to say of certain young women that for a ride they would part with their honour, then one might aptly vary the phrase and say: for a pass, with everything.

There are human beings, persons with so-called "good connections," who lead a wonderful life with the aid of passes. The physician who is at their beck and call throughout the year is compensated for his efforts by the presentation from time to time of a box or a pair of seats for the theatre. So, too, the lawyer. The Cerberus rage of the most terrifying of all apartment-house superintendents melts into the gentlest humility at the prospect of a pass. We expect a thousand little favours from our fellow-citizens who assume the obligation to render these favours by the acceptance of a pass.

There are probably only very few persons who feel any shame on going on a trip with a pass. These exceptional beings have not yet discovered that nowadays it is only the person who pays who is looked down upon. Every one takes his hat off to the possessor of a pass. The train conductor makes a respectful bow because he does not know whether the "dead-head" is an officer of the company or some other "big gun." The ticket collector does the same because experience has taught him that the dead-head usually overcomes by a treat the social inferiority associated with "enjoyment without payment." In short, a pass invests its possessor with the mysterious air of a great power and weaves about his head a halo which lifts him above the *misers plebs contribuens.*

But you must not think that the possessor of passes constitutes that part of the public that is particularly grateful for and appreciative of the artistic offerings. On the contrary! Artistic enjoyment in the theatre requires a certain capacity for illusion, and the purchase of a ticket exercises a considerable influence on this capacity. For one who has dearly paid for his seat has imposed the moral obligation upon himself to be entertained.

Down in his subliminal self there dwell forces that may be said to have been lessoned to applaud. The higher the price, the more painfully the pleasure was purchased, the greater is the willingness to be carried away by the work of art and the artists. The poor student who has stood for hours in front of the opera house and been lucky enough to secure admission to standing room in the gallery will have a better time than his rich colleague down in the orchestra, and a very much better time than the envied possessor of a free seat. For his capacity for illusion has been tremendously heightened. He expects a reward commensurate with the trouble he went to and the money he sacrificed. His tension being much higher, the relaxation of that tension must yield him a much greater quantity of pleasure. The greater the restraints that one has to overcome the greater the pleasure in having succeeded in overcoming them.

The necessity for illusion is absent in the possessor of a pass. There is nothing to make it incumbent on him to be entertained; he has not paid anything. He can even leave the performance before it is concluded if it does not please him. He is more sceptical, more critical, and less grateful.

Any dramatist who at a *première* would fill the theatre with his good friends by giving them passes would have little knowledge of human nature; certain failure would await him. Not only because these so-called good friends, in obedience to their unconscious envy, frankly join the enemy's ranks, but because the possessors of passes involuntarily get into the psychic condition which is characteristic of "dead-heads," viz: indifferent critical smugness and a diminished capacity for illusion.

I know of a striking example of this that came under my own observation. One of my friends, a young playwright, invited his tailor and his wife to go to his *première*, and not to be backward in expressing their approval. He had distributed a sufficiently large number of friends in the orchestra, but the gallery had not been provided for. He had, naturally, also sent two tickets to one of his competitors. It so chanced that I was in the thick of it, because I was interested in seeing how the simple public would receive the piece. I sat right behind the doughty tailor couple, who, of course, did not know me. Several times during the performance we almost came to blows. The married couple hissed with might and main, whereas I applauded with all my power. We exchanged angry words and otherwise acted in a manner characteristic of such a situation and of such a youthful temper as mine then was. The play was a failure. Later we discussed the reason for this failure. One said that the play was not deep enough for the enlightened public. I challenged this contention, and referred to the simple people who sat in front of me and whose names and station I had discovered from some neighbours. My friend would not believe me at first until I had convinced him by a detailed description of the couple that the tailor who had for so many years made his clothes had felt it incumbent on him to repay the author's gift of a pass by contributing to the failure of his play.

To be under obligations always oppresses us. We have the instinctive impulse to disregard them. A pass is an obligation to acknowledge the excellence of the offered entertainment, to confirm that it is worth the price of admission. In addition to the absence of a need for illusion from material considerations we have to reckon with the impulse to disregard this obligation. These two psychic factors serve to bring about in the heart of the possessor of a pass the defence reaction that I have previously described.

Notwithstanding this, the craving for passes, which formerly was the privilege of the few exceptional personages, keeps growing more and more, infecting other levels of society, and would easily become a serious menace to the directorate of the theatres if these had not hit upon an adequate remedy in distributing passes on the homœpathic principle. They fight the "pass with the pass." They distribute passes and reduced rate tickets very lavishly for the days on which they know the receipts will be poor and for plays which no longer draw large audiences. The exaction of a small fee on the presentation of the coupon serves to cover part of the running expenses; the house is filled and the many's fire for passes is quenched. On the following days the people are much more willing to buy their tickets because they think that they can afford to be so extravagant, inasmuch as they had seen one or more performances free or practically so, and are swayed by the unconscious instinct that a purchased pleasure is sure to prove more delightful.

One would have to be a second limping Mephisto to be able to follow the invisible stream of passes in a large metropolis. The romance of a pass is still to be written. It would yield us an insight into the psychology of modern man that would be second to none. It would prove that one of the most important impulses of our time is the desire not to have to work for one's pleasures. I say "not to work for one's pleasures" rather than "not to pay for one's pleasures," because money always means an equivalent for our work. The most industrious persons are in reality those who are most averse to work. For behind their zeal to accummulate money there is the burning desire to hoard up as much as will ensure an income sufficient to purchase enjoyment without additional work. In the language of every day this would be: a care-free old age. But, in sooth, worry is the main source of our pleasures. Were there no cares the variegated colours of the spectrum that constitute the light of life would be replaced by dull monotonous grays that resemble each other as closely as the two links that unite the two ends of a chain converting it into a whole.

The pursuit after passes is only a small fragment of that mad pursuit after "pleasure without work" that is being enacted all around us. I have gone into the subject so minutely only because it is a typical example of mankind's stupid beginning to free itself from the iron bonds of material dependence. For the more free we think ourselves, the more enslaved we really are.

IDENTIFICATION

I know a man who suffered a great deal from his wife's moods. No matter how much he tried he could never please her. If he was happy and contented she called him "Mr. Frivolous" and would say what a fine figure he'd cut in a Punch and Judy show; if, on the contrary, cares troubled him and his face betrayed his anxiety, she called him "Old Grouch" and railed at him for making her life bitter. If he wanted to go to the theatre, she thought they ought to stay home; if he longed for the peace of the home, she egged him on to take part in all sorts of senseless pastimes. Is it any wonder that the poor man became "nervous"? that he lost his peace of mind and his hitherto imperturbable good humour?

In those painful days his comfort was his quiet daughter who seemed to be in all respects the opposite of her moody mother. He sought sanctuary with her, and over and over again she had to listen to his cries for peace.

Finally his nervous condition got so bad that a physician had to be consulted. The physician being fully aware of the patient's domestic relations did not have to consider very long and ordered the sick man to take a trip. More easily prescribed than done. For our patient had one very bad habit: he could not be alone. It was a cruel punishment for him to have to look after his small daily wants away from home. What was he to do? His wife would gladly have gone along with him. But there were numerous objections to that. Besides, the wise physician would not hear of it. In this quandary the distressed man thought of his gentle, affectionate, young daughter. Everybody rejoiced at this happy solution; the anxious physician, the jealous wife, and, not least, the sensible daughter who had not yet seen anything of the world and whose secret dreams of youth had been disturbed by the erratic educational methods of her mother, in which exaggerated love and pitiless sternness alternated.

Great excitement marked the time for departure. Mother changed her plans ten times over. First she wanted to drop everything and accompany her husband; then she wanted to induce the unhappy husband to give up the trip, and so on. Finally the time for departure arrived. They were on the platform at the station and were saying the last good-byes. Mother had an unlimited number of things to say and suggestions to make. Then the conductor gave the last warning and there was no time to lose. Through the little window the happy father and the still happier daughter looked out on the source of their woes who had been suddenly converted into an inexhaustible fountain of tears. Was she so grieved because the objects upon whom she was wont to project the discontent of her unresting heart were gone? With a sudden movement she wiped away her tears and called after her daughter in stentorian tones: "Freda, now you'll take the place of your mother! Remember that!"—What else she said was lost in the din of the moving train whose shrill whistle drowned the asthmatic woman's commanding tones. During the next few seconds they waved their last greetings and then the scene so painful to all was over.

Father and daughter looked at each other, their faces beaming. For a little while, at any rate, they would be free and have nothing else to do but to enjoy life. The mother's last words rang in their ears. Involuntarily the man smiled and remarked tenderly to his daughter: "Well—I shall be curious to see how my little sunshine will take her mother's place." The little one looked at her father seriously and replied: "Papa, I shall try to do so to the best of my power, surely." And deep within her she rejoiced at the thought that strangers might think her really the young wife of this fine-looking man.

After a few minutes Freda began to complain that it was getting very cold. "There is a draught! It's terribly cold!" The anxious father at once closed the window. After a little while she complained that the compartment was unbearably stuffy. Why had not the conductor assigned them a more spacious one? Had papa given him a tip? She had been told by a friend who had just returned from a wedding trip in Italy that conductors are respectful and accommodating only to those who give liberal tips. She was not so inexperienced as a certain papa seemed to think. If he gave the man the tip they would surely be transferred to a more comfortable car. Somewhat irritated, the father complied with his daughter's wish. After considerable trouble they were transferred from their small cosy compartment in which they could sit alone, to a large one into which a stout elderly gentleman entered at the next station and plumped himself down beside them. Freda had an insurmountable repugnance to fat old gentlemen. She reproached her father; he had not given the conductor a large enough tip.

Why waste words? After a few hours the poor man saw only too clearly that his daughter was bent on taking her mother's place in the true sense of the word. She pestered him with her moods and gave him not a minute's rest. He tried to console himself with the thought that Freda was not herself owing to the excitement of the last few days, and that she would soon be herself again. Vain hope! The girl was as if transformed. From a quiet, amiable child, she had become a moody, fractious torment. The trip which had been intended as a cure became an unmitigable torture. For at home he knew how to adapt himself quietly to his wife's tyranny. But here, away from home, he was constantly getting into all sorts of unpleasant situations. Finally, he pretended to be too sick to continue the trip and after a few days they returned home.

I have narrated this tragic-comical history in such detail because it makes the meaning of "Identification" clearer than any definition could. What had happened to the young girl to transform her so quickly? Her mother had enjoined her to take her place. She had to some extent taken upon herself her mother's duties. She identified herself with her mother. She played the role of mother exactly as she had for years seen it played at home, though, in secret, she had disapproved of her mother's conduct. This identification nullified her own personality and replaced it with another.

This is a phenomenon that takes the most suprising forms among the victims of hysteria. But it would be erroneous to think that it occurs only among hysterics. Almost all persons, especially women, succumb to the seductive power of identification. I wonder if it is because of this that all of us secretly bear a measure of neurosis with us throughout life! At home, Freda might have concealed her hysteria as a kind of reaction to her mother's conduct. It was only when she had to play the mother's role that the neurosis, in consequence of an unconscious affect, became manifest. It is thus that epidemics of hysteria break out. If a neurosis is capable of transferring an affect, it can arouse another, slumbering neurosis. For to-day we know, from Bleuler's studies, that suggestion is not the transference of an idea but an affect.

The phenomenon that the above case brings out so clearly and unequivocally may be seen in everyday life behind various motives, catch-words, tendencies, and strivings. Notwithstanding these disguises the eye of the investigator will not find it difficult to recognize the mechanism of identification and the element of the neurosis in the normal person. But if this is so everybody is neurotic. Let us not get excited about this conclusion. There is no such thing as a normal human being. What we call disease and abnormality are only the highest peaks of a mountain chain that rises to various heights above the sea-level of the normal. Every person has his weak spots, physical and psychical. We can reckon only relative heights, never the absolute, inasmuch as a standard of the normal is really never at our disposal.

There is no difficulty in finding illustrations of the process of identification in the so-called normal. Take, for example, the valet of the nobleman. How thoroughly imbued he is with his master's pride of ancestry! With what imperturbable scorn he looks down upon the common rabble! It never enters his mind that he is one of the masses. He has no glimmer of appreciation of the absurdity of his airs, because the mechanism of identification has clouded his intellect and an emotion has strangled his logic. He even gives verbal expression to his feeling of identification. He seems to have become fused into a unity with his master, for he submerges his individuality, his ego, and on every occasion speaks of "we" and "us."

"We are starting south to-day," he announces to the neighbours. "We shall stay home," he declares oracularly to visitors.

We see the same thing in the school child. It takes a little time before he can free himself from the influence of his teachers and of the school. Not infrequently he cannot do so owing to the permanent fixation of his identification with them. Horace's "Jurare in verba magistri" (*i.e.*, to echo the sentiments of one's master) is nothing but the result of a completely successful identification. One who cannot free himself from this affect and substitute for the confident "we" of the school the uncertain "I" of individuality can never hope to become an independent personality.

Some feelings, such as so-called party spirit, pride of ancestry, solidarity, national pride, etc., are only identifications. The German identifies himself with his great national heroes, e.g., Schiller, Goethe, Bismarck, etc., and is then as proud of being a German as if that implied that he had himself been responsible for their great achievements. The well-known and almost ridiculous pride of the Englishman is only the product of an extreme identification. But, as a matter of fact, the British Government also identifies itself with the humblest of its subjects and protects him in whatever corner of the earth he may happen to be. The officer who takes great pride in his regiment, the pupil who is all enthusiasm for the colours of his school, and the ordinary citizen who can see no element of goodness in any but his own political party, all bear witness to the great power of identification. It is in this way that socialism has become such a tremendous power. Not because it furnishes the proletariat with a dream of a happier future, not because it has supplied it with a religion. (The Church supplies this want better.) No! Only because it has enabled the individual, the weak one, to feel himself one with a tremendous majority, to identify himself with an organization that is world-wide. Socialism is the triumph of identification and the death-knell of individualism.

The most beautiful instance of identification is furnished by love. One who is in love has completely identified himself with the beloved. "Two souls with but a single thought; two hearts that beat as one." Has not Rückert designated his beloved as his "better self"? (Or Kletke's very popular song: "What is thine and what is mine?") A lover almost literally transfers his whole ego into another's soul. He projects all his yearning upon that one object. He is oblivious of his mistakes until the identification is over. Then the intoxicating dream, too, is over.

With the aid of identification a lover can transfer his passion upon any object that stands in some sort of relationship to his beloved. It is in this way that fetichism sometimes results. That is why love for a woman so easily leads to a love for her kindred. There is a Slavic proverb which says: "He who loves his wife also cherishes his mother-in-law." And, on the other hand, a discontent with one's wife is often concealed behind a stubborn hatred of her relatives. In many instances the feeling against mothers-in-law cannot be interpreted in any other way.

Thus there runs through the soul of mankind an endless chain of identifications ranging from the normal to the pathological. The child that puts its father's hat on its head identifies itself with him just as certainly as the lunatic who thinks himself Napoleon. Both have realized their wishes. But there is this difference between them: In the normal the identification is held under control by the force of facts, whereas in the lunatic the identification has suffered a fixation. A delusion is frequently only a wholly successful identification in the interests of the desire to escape from painful realities. Delusion and truth are plastic conceptions. Who could presume to define where truth ceases and delusion begins? From

Schopenhauer's point of view our whole world-philosophy might be said to be only a process of identification. And truth is nothing but the transference of our own limited knowledge upon the outer world.

REFUGE IN DISEASE

The psychological study of disease is still, alas! a very young and immature science. We have been held so long in the thrall of the materialistic delusion of having to look for bacilli and other micro-organisms behind all diseases that we have almost wholly neglected the psychic factor in disease. It now seems that these psychic factors play the chief role in the so-called "nervous" diseases, whereas all the other "causes," namely, the predisposition, heredity, infection, etc., it now turns out, do play a certain role, not an unimportant one, it is true, but yet a secondary one. The influence of emotional disturbance upon these diseases has only recently received careful study.

We have learned that psychic causes may play a great role in the occurrence and the prevention of disease. We may confidently assert that without the presence of a psychic component which invokes the disease hardly a single case of nervous disease could occur. Paradoxical as this may sound it is nearer the truth than the orthodox teachings of our day. For who does not recollect times in his childhood when he longed to be sick that he might not have to go to school, and that he might at the same time be petted and indulged by his parents? A little of this infantilism persists with us throughout life. Hysterics especially are distinguished by the infantilism of their thoughts, their feelings, and their ideas. This being so, we must agree with Bleuler when he asserts that the most common cause of hysteria is the desire to take refuge in disease. It will be of interest here to reproduce Bleuler's report of one of his cases (from his book on "affectivity, suggestibility, and paranoia," published by Karl Marhold in 1906).

"A *paterfamilias* suffers an injury in a railway accident. How terrible it would be if he were so disabled that he could no longer provide for his family and if he had to go through life that way, suffering all the time, and half the time unable to work! How much better it would be if he were dead or wholly disabled. His attorney informs him that his annual earnings equal the interest on 80,000 francs, and that he could bring an action for that amount—a sum which would insure his family against want for the rest of their lives. Are there not indications enough that he will need this sum? Isn't it a fact that he is already suffering from insomnia? Work fatigues him—his head aches—railway journeys make him apprehensive and even cause attacks of anxiety; how helpful it would be, nay, how absolutely necessary it would be, to prove that he is very sick and to get that 80,000 francs! And now the traumatic neurosis or psychosis is established, and will in all probability not be curable until the lawsuit is satisfactorily settled." Bleuler does not mince matters but roundly asserts that in this case the wish caused the neurosis. Would it be proper to call these people malingerers? By no means! For, naturally, all these wishes are not clearly known to these individuals; they suffer in good faith. The wish emanates from unconscious levels. Consciousness vehemently resents any imputation of the thought of simulation. Such invalids usually protest vehemently their desire to be well. "How happy would I be if only I had my health! Then I would gladly dispense with damages!"

Here I should like to report two cases from my own experience which serve to illustrate the refuge in disease even better than the case described by the distinguished Swiss psychiatrist. The first was a very sick woman who had been bed-ridden for six years. No organic malady could be discovered. The diagnosis was hysteria. The deeper cause of her malady was as follows: Her husband was a coarse, brutal fellow, continually upbraiding her for something or other and raising fearful rows; but when she was sick his whole nature underwent a change. Then he became amiable, affectionate and attentive. As soon as she was well he became the old, unendurable, domestic tyrant. Finally, there was nothing for this delicate, weak woman to do but to take refuge in disease.

Her limbs used to tremble and refuse their function, so that she had to stay in bed or be rolled about in an invalid chair. All the skill of her physicians—and she had the best the metropolis had to offer—proved unavailing. Naturally the cure of such a case is hardly possible unless one can remove the cause for the refuge in disease. In this case this solution was out of the question, and so the woman goes on enjoying the blessed fruits of her invalidism, complainingly but not unhappily, exulting within, but miserable without.

Our everyday life furnishes numerous petty examples of refuge in disease: the nervous wife who breaks out in a hysterical crying spell if her husband reproaches her; the schoolboy who complains of headache when he cannot get his lessons done; the husband who gets pains in the stomach every time his wife makes life unbearable;—they all take refuge in disease as a means of escape from their persecutor. How often is this phenomenon observed among soldiers, for whom a few days of illness means the most delightful change! In these cases even the most experienced military physicians often find it impossible to distinguish between wish and reality.

A physician who does not know of the phenomenon we have designated as "refuge in disease" will be helpless in the handling of most cases of hysteria. A blooming young girl had for two years consulted specialists of the highest repute about the raging headaches with which she was afflicted. All the usual remedies, such as antipyrin, phenacetin, pyramidon, and even morphine, failed to give her even slight temporary relief. The experts thought of a tumor in the brain and of other dangerous maladies as the possible cause of these obstinate headaches. But it turned out that this headache, too, was only a refuge in disease. A casual remark of the father's betrayed the true nature of the trouble: "My daughter is about to be married; she has been engaged for two years, and the young man is anxiously waiting for the wedding; but I can't let her marry while she is suffering from such a severe disease."

The headache was obviously the means of getting out of a hateful marriage. Of course one who would have been content with her first story would never have discovered the truth. What stories she told about her wonderful love! How ardently she loved her betrothed! There was nothing she longed for more than the wedding-day! How unhappy she would be if she lost him! But a careful psychanalysis brought forth ample and convincing comfirmation of the above-mentioned suspicion. The girl had been engaged once before; in fact she had not yet completely broken off her relations with her former lover. In addition thereto there were confessions about the death of all erotic feelings during the second engagement, as to which we cannot go into details. It was quite clear that her malady was a refuge in invalidism. I advised breaking the engagement. The advice was not followed. On the contrary, the family hoped that a speedy marriage might bring about a cure of the hysterical condition. But the young woman is still going about, complaining and whimpering, with her malady (from which her husband, notwithstanding his inexhaustible patience, suffers more than she). Will she ever be well? If she ever learns to love her husband she may recover her health. But where such powerful, unconscious counter-impulses, such powerful instincts, contend against an inclination, it is scarcely possible that this inclination will develop into full sovereignty of the soul.

What we have just said of the neurosis is also true of the delusions of insanity. A delusion also is a fleeing from this world into another one in which some particular over-valued idea represses all other ideas and dominates the mind. It will not be long ere this conception will be an accepted doctrine of all psychiatrists. For the time being it is the common property of creative literary artists, who, because of their intuitive insight into human nature, have frequently given expression to this idea. It is perhaps most beautifully expressed by Georges Rodenbach, the Flemish artist, unfortunately too early deceased, who says in one of his fine posthumous novels ("Die Erfüllung," Dresden, 1905):—

"The insane have nothing to complain of. Often they achieve their purposes only in this way. They become what they have longed for and what they would otherwise never have become. They obtain the coveted goal and their plans are fulfilled. They live what once they dreamed. Their delusion is, to all intents and purposes, their inner fruition, inasmuch as it corresponds to their most ardent desires and their most secret yearnings. Thus the ambitious one ascends in his delusions the heights that have beckoned to him ; he possesses endless treasures, orders the destinies of great nations, and moves only among the great rulers of the earth. Religious delusion brings its victim to the throne of God and makes life in Paradise a tangible reality. So that delusion always realises the goal that each has longed for. It gratifies our desires to the utmost limit. Sympathetically it takes a hand in our affairs and completes the altogether too pretentious destiny of those upon whom fulfillment never smiles."

What a beautiful idea ! Delusion is a wish-fulfilment exactly as the dream is. The madhouse is the paradise of thoughts, the heaven in which wishes meet with unlimited fulfilment. And human beings sicken so often, and madness increases with such uncanny rapidity, because our most secret wishes are never gratified, because in these dull times the miraculous has died, and because life demands so much renunciation and yields so little happiness.

Let us draw these lessons from the foregoing remarks: to keep one's desires within bounds means to assure one's spiritual health. Inordinate ambition, which foolish parents kindle in their children's hearts, is often the cause of an early breakdown. We must school ourselves and our children to wish only for the attainable and to attain our desires. Our ideals must live in our breasts, not in the outer world. Then we may find in ourselves what the world denies us. They who can find refuge in their health will escape having to take refuge in disease.

WHY WE TRAVEL

Why do we not know why we travel ? Haven't we the imperative obligation to recuperate ? Does not our malady enforce a trip to a health resort ? Are we not thirsty for new countries, new people, a new environment ?

Peace ! peace ! No, we do not know ! Or rather, we do not wish to know. Naturally, we always have a few superficial motives at our disposal when it suits us to mask our unconscious secrets from ourselves and from the world. Why do we travel ? Psychologists have given many reasons, but they do not go beyond such superficial motives as "the desire for a change," "a craving for excitement," "curiosity," "fatigue, the need for a rest," "flight from the home," etc. Some go further and attribute the desire to travel to the elementary pleasure of being in motion. For these psychologists the little child's first step is its first journey, the last step of the weary aged their last journey. Others again veritably classify journeys and distinguish between trips undertaken for health reasons, business trips, scientific trips, etc.

Vain beginning ! In reality one trip is like another. If we would understand the elementary feelings associated with a trip we must go back to our youth. In youth we still have a sense of the wonderful; in youth the horizon of our fantasies is aglow with wondrous visions. But of course the world about us is solemn and wearisome, full of duties and obligations. But ah, the wide world without! There dangerous adventures smile alluringly; there unrestrained freedom beckons; there deeds may be achieved that may make kings of us. In our thoughts we build a small skiff that will take us out of the narrow channel of our homes into the vast sea; we battle on the prairie with the brave and crafty Indians; we seek out the sun-burned gold-fields in the new world; we put a hurried girdle round about the earth, and—when at top speed—we would even attempt a flight to the moon.

Nothing that makes an impression on the human mind is ever lost. Our youth with its fantasies and childish desires exerts an important influence on us all our life. Henceforth all our excursions are journeys into the realm of youth. All, all are alike. Life hems us in with innumerable obstacles, bonds, and walls. The older we grow the greater becomes the weight that loads us down. In the depths of the soul the tintinnabulation of youth is ringing and speaking to us of life and freedom, and keeps on ringing alluringly till weary man surrenders and takes a trip. The tinkling music of the soul works strongest on the mind of youth. He, fortunate he, knows not the difference between the music of his heart and the hum of the world without. He knows not yet that the world is everywhere the same, the people everywhere the same, and the mountains, the lakes, the seas, with but slight variations, the same. His longings carry him out, far out, and he seeks their fulfilment.

The adult lives a life of bitter disappointments. He never seeks the new. He longs only to get rid of the old. And the aged wanderer, having reached the end of the vale of life, follows his buried wishes, his memories of the beautiful days in which there was still something to hope for, in which he was not beyond self-deception.

It is not to be denied that ours is *the* travelling age. This is partly due to the fact that we experience so little, as we have already said, in our craving for excitement. The many inventions that have conquered time and space have made it possible for us to fly over the whole world, and thus the primary purpose of travelling, the hunger for experience, shrinks into trivial, merry or vexatious hotel adventures. But in every such trip one may discover a deeply hidden kernel of the voyages of the old Vikings. Every journey is a tour of conquest. Here at home we have found our level; our neighbours know us and have passed their irrevocable judgment on our person. To travel means to conquer the world anew, to make oneself respected and esteemed. Every new touring acquaintance must stand for a new conquest. We display all our talents for which we no longer have any use at home and all our almost rusty intellectual weapons, our amiability, our courteousness, our gallantry, are again taken out of the soul's lumber chamber and put to use in conquering new persons. This secret foolery compensates us for all the plans of conquest that we have long ago given up. To conquer persons without having to depend on one's social background is one of the greatest delights of travelling.

How strange! As in ordinary life we seek ourself and are overjoyed to find ourself in our environment and get most out of the individual who is most like ourself, so everywhere abroad we seek our own home. How happy we are on beholding a familiar face even though it be that of a person who has been ever so unsympathetic or indifferent. We are delighted with him and greet him like a trusted friend—only because he represents for us a fragment of our home which we have been seeking out here and which we have found, to some extent, in him. That is why such discoveries make us happiest as revealing identities with our home. Even in this the infantile character of travelling is shown. Just as in our youth we had to learn many things that we had to forget subsequently so we act with regard to our journeys; every new city, every new region is a kind of primer whose fundamentals we have to make our own no matter how much it goes against our grain to do so. The faithful visiting of all the objects of interest with our Baedeker in our hands, the profound sense of an obligation to have seen so-and-so is clearly such an infantile trait and has about it much of the youthfulness and school-boyishness of the time in which the teacher's authority meant compelling knowledge to follow a set norm.

Much might be said about the technique of travelling. The manner in which the thought springs from the unconscious, gently and with tender longing, takes on more definite shape and apparently suddenly breaks out during the night with the violence of a deed, presents almost a neurotic picture, and one is justified, from this point of view, in speaking of a "touring neurosis." Every repression begets a compulsive idea. The repression of the emotions of youth begets a touring neurosis. The compulsion is strongest in the first few days during which difficult internal conflicts have to be overcome. The threads that bind us to our home, our vocation, and our beloved, must first be wholly severed. This happens only after several days, after the so-called "travel-reaction." That is the name I would propose for that unpleasant feeling that overcomes us after a few days. Suddenly we feel lonesome and alone, curse the desire that prompted us to leave our home, and play with the idea whether it would not be better to terminate the trip and go back home. It is only when this reaction has been overcome, when the conflict between the present and the past has been decided in favour of the latter, only then has one acquired the correct attitude to travelling, an attitude which depends upon a complete forgetting of our social and individual obligations. It is, for all the world, as if after this reaction we had suppressed all our relations to our home and freed all our inhibitions. Only then can we enjoy the pleasure of travelling, but, alas, it lasts only a short time. For soon there rises before our eyes, like a threatening monster, the time when we must again resume our obligations. The sense of duty gets stronger and stronger, the desire for travelling gets weaker and weaker, and after a short but decisive conflict, the fever for travelling abates, leaving behind it a little heap of ashes in which the feeble coals of memory gradually die.

It is a profound feeling of bliss that we feel at home, for down at the bottom of the heart we have always been faithful to the home. We see everything in the new colours with which our journey has beautified the dull gray of daily life; alas! they are only temporary joys, borrowed harmonies, which lose their intensity in the day's progress and are bound to return to their former dulness.

Particular mention must be made of the journeys of married couples. These, too, are trips into the realm of youth, into the beautiful country of the bethrothal period, and thus every such trip is a new honeymoon. The energies which had hitherto been devoted to the discharge of their duties have now been freed and burst powerfully into the amatory sphere ; but they may also intensify components of aversion and hatred, and are just as likely to emphasize antagonisms as, under circumstances, they may build bridges over bottomless depths. Inasmuch as *en tour* thought and feeling are dominated by infantile traits, and inasmuch as to a certain extent a new spring of love awakens with the youthful fire and youthful tenderness, a journey may—just because of these results—result in disappointments such as cannot otherwise be brought to light in staid old age.

Let us also make mention of the opportunity a journey gives one of living a purely physical existence, of enjoying the rare pleasure of feeling oneself a creature of muscles, a thing all backbone and little brain. Let us also mention the delight of feeling oneself a stranger, of shaking off every irritating constraint, of being able to break with impunity the rules of propriety and good breeding, and we have, in comparison with all the really important psychological motives, touched only a small part of the surface psychology of travelling.

And now I come to the really important point of my thesis. What I have hitherto said is of general validity, applying to the generality of travelling people. But I believe that every individual has also a secret, deep-lying motive of which he himself is unaware and which one rarely is in a position to discover. Now and then one may succeed in discovering such a motive and one is then astonished at the strange things that may be hidden behind the passion of travelling.

There are so many things that we seek all our life and that, alas! we can never find. One is on the hunt for a friend who will "understand" him; another for a beloved whom he can comprehend; the third for a place where he may find the people he has dreamed of. Which of us has not his secret, dark desires and longings which really belong to "the other one" within us and not to the outer personage on whom the sun shines? What is denied us by the environment may possibly be found somewhere beyond. What withers here may bear luxuriant blossoms somewhere beyond. . .

The deepest-lying, repressed desires are the driving power in the fever for travelling. We are infected—infected by the seeds that have been slumbering within us for years and which have now with mysterious power engendered the ardour that drives us on to travel. Behind every journey there lies a hidden motive. It will, of course, be a difficult matter to discover in every case this deeply hidden motive, this innermost spring of action. In some cases one succeeds, however, and lights upon most remarkable things. One may hit upon some exciting touring experience of earlier days, upon a strange fantasy, upon some sweet wish that seems to be too grotesque to be spoken of openly.

No one has yet fathomed just what constitutes happiness. It is never the present, always the future. A trip is a journey into the future, a hunting after happiness.

The best light on the psychology of the "touring neurosis" is thrown by a consideration of the opposite phenomenon—the "fear of travelling." There are many persons who are afraid of every journey, for whom a railroad trip is a torture, for whom going away from home is a punishment. There are persons who have compromised with the present and have given up all hope of a future; who have no happiness to lose and therefore have no wish to achieve any; who fear any great change and who have become wrapped up in themselves. They are the great panegyrists of home, the enthusiastic patriots, the contemners of everything foreign. They behave exactly like the fox for whom the grapes were too sour. Because their fears won't let them travel they prove to themselves and to the world at large that travelling is nonsensical, that the city they live in is the best of all places to live in. The fear of travelling also has a hidden motive which not rarely is fortified by justifiable and unjustifiable consciousness of guilt. Why we do not travel is often a much more interesting problem than why we do travel.

Fear and desire are brother and sister and emanate from the same primal depths. The wish often converts to fear and fear to wish.

One who is incapable in his heart to fly from himself and his environment bears a heavy and unbreakable chain within his soul. So do we all. But we break it now and then. The future may perhaps create free human beings. Then there may perhaps be no abysms of the soul. Just at present darkness surrounds us. The mysteries of the soul are barred to us. Its depths are unfathomable. Even if we have illumined some hidden corner and brought something that was long concealed to the light of consciousness, it is only like a drop snatched from the infinity of the ocean. The real reason why we travel can be told us only by our " other self," that " other one " whom we buried in our remote youth. Whither we travel is quite clear. Large and small, young and old, fools and wise men—all journey to the realm of youth. Life takes us into the kingdom of dreams, and the dream takes us back again into life, into that life to which we have been assigned and to which our deepmost desires belong. What desires ? Those are the secrets we anxiously conceal from ourselves.

MOODY PERSONS

A beautiful warm summer day. The churchyard lies dreamily in the sultry noonday atmosphere. All nature seems to be possessed by the desire to imitate the sleep of those interred in the womb of earth. Suddenly there is heard a grinding sound in the fine gravel and a curly, rosy-cheeked, dark-haired lad is seen leaping over hedges and over mounds after a gilded butterfly . . .

Wondrous images loom up before me like large great question marks in the trembling air. Similar scenes from the distant mirage of my own youth come to mind. Like a hot, long-dammed-up stream my emotions break from the unconsciousness into consciousness. I am overcome by a long-forgotten yearning. Is not my heart beating faster? Is there not a wild pleasure in the melancholy that oppresses me?

How strange! A little while ago I lay lost in cheerful reflections in the tall grass, delighting in the noiseless pace of time, and now I am excited, restless, disturbed, and sad, but not unhappy. My mood has undergone a complete change. What has brought this transformation about? Surely, only the appearance of the beautiful boy who was trying to catch a butterfly with his green net. Why did this scene excite me so? There must have been set up in my mind a thinking process of which I was not conscious. Some secret power that drives the wheels of the emotions had set into action a long-inhibited and hidden spring.

Gradually the shadowy thoughts came into the bright light of comprehension. The boy was to me a symbol of my life. An echo of my distant youth. And the slumbering cemetery, my inevitable future. My heart too is a cemetery. Numberless buried hopes, too early slain, unblown buds, longings goaded to death, unfulfilled wishes lie buried here within and no cross betrays their presence. And over all these dead possibilities I, too, am chasing a gilded butterfly. And when I catch it in my net I seize it with my rude heavy hands, doing violence to the delicate dust on its wings, and throw the lusterless remainders among the dead. Or it is destined to a place in a box, transfixed with the fine needle named "impression" and constituting one of the collection of dead butterflies which go to make up "memory."

It really was an "unconscious" thought, then, that transformed my mood from *dur* into *moll*. And the truth dawns on me that all our "incomprehensible" moods are logical and that they must all have a secret psychic motivation. Moody persons are persons with whom things are not in order. Their consciousness is split up into numerous emotionally-toned "complexes." An unconscious complex is like a state within a state. A sovereign power, too repressed, too weak, and too tightly fettered to break into consciousness without having to unmask, but strong enough to influence the individual's conduct. Moody persons have their good and their bad days. The bad days are incomprehensible puzzles to them. Simple souls speak of being under the influence of demons; poets share their pains with the rest of the world and "sublimate" their petty individual woes into a gigantic world-woe; commonplace souls place the responsibility for their moods upon "nature," the bad weather, the boss, the husband, or wife, their cook, their employment, and what not.

In the grasp of an incomprehensible mood we are ill at ease and anxious, very much like a brave person who finds himself threatened in a dark forest by a vindictive enemy whom he cannot see. To muster up courage we deceive ourselves, just as the little child that falteringly proclaims: "Please, please! I am good. The bogey man won't come!" But the bogey man does come, for a certainty. He always comes again because everything that is repressed must take on the characteristics of a psychic compulsion. If we do not want him to come again we must bravely raise our eyelids and look at him fixedly with eyes of understanding and realise that he is nothing but a phantom of our excited senses, that he does not exist and has not existed. The bogey man cannot long endure this penetrating look; slowly he dissolves into grey shadows and disappears for ever.

Modern psychologists have pointed out the relationship between unmotived moods and the periodical character of certain phenomena of life. It is, of course, a fact that we are all subject to certain partly known and partly unknown periodical influences. But whether this alone is sufficient reason for attacks of depression does not seem to me to have been proved. My own experiences speak against it. Just as a stone, thrown into a body of water, causes the appearance of broad circular ripples which gradually get feebler and feebler until they disappear with a scarcely perceptible undulation of the surface, so does a strong impression continue to work within us, giving rise to ever wider but ever feebler circles. Only when these circles set a floating mine in motion does the water shoot up, the mud is thrown on high, and the clear surface is muddied. These floating mines are the split off, unconscious complexes. The secret thought must not be put in motion.

But enough of metaphors! Let us take an example from our daily life. A women is suffering from frequently-recurring incomprehensible depressions. She has everything that a childish, spoiled heart can desire. And she is not a spoiled child, for she had been a poor seamstress when she made her husband's acquaintance. Now she lives in a magnificent palace, wears costly garments, has a houseful of servants, adorns herself with the finest laces ; her husband clothes her like a doll, pampers and coddles her, treats her with the greatest affection—in short, worships her. And this woman, the envy of her associates as she rides by them in her splendid automobile, has days on which she cries for hours. Our first guess is she does not love her husband. You are wrong, you psychologists of the old school ! She does love her husband, she is as happy with her finery and wealth as a child with a toy ; she can assign no cause for her melancholy.

Notwithstanding this, her depression was of pyschic origin. When we investigated carefully the experiences and excitements that ushered in one of these attacks it became clear that subterranean bridges led to secret (suppressed) desires. Quite often the immediate occasion was of a trifling nature. She had seen a poor woman pass her in the street. Alone ? No—with a young man, very happy, care-free, their arms affectionately intertwined. On another occasion she had been reading of a pair of lovers who had drowned themselves. Suicide was a subject, beyond all others, which she could not bear to hear. At the theatre she once sat in a box on the third tier. Suddenly she looked down into the orchestra and was seized with horror. That was a yawning abyss ! What if her opera glass fell down there ! Or if she lost her balance and toppled over! A shudder passed through her. She put the opera glass aside and became greatly depressed.

The mystery surrounding her melancholy was soon solved. Her husband, fifteen years her senior, is not adapted to her temperamentally. In secret she longs for a life rich in emotions, full of sin and perhaps also of vice. Nature probably intended her for a fast woman, not for an eminently respectable lady. Alluring melodies beckon her to the metropolis. She would rather lose her breath in an endless dance in the tight embrace of a pair of coarse arms than ride sedately down the main avenue. She loves her husband, but sometimes she hates him. He's the obstacle. She knows how terribly jealous he is. He was very sick once; just then the wicked thought entered her mind: "If he died now I'd be rich and free!" The reaction was not long in coming. She saw herself as a dreadful sinner. Life had no more interest for her. Since then she has been suffering from periodical attacks of depression.

What happened in this case in the wake of powerful repressions happens a little in all moody persons. An unconscious motive for the depression can always be demonstrated. In most instances it is secret reproaches that provoke the change in mood. In young people they are the sequel of exaggerated warnings about not injuring their health. Sins against religion and morality. Reproaches for too readily yielding to one's impulses. But also the opposite!

Many an attack of depression is nothing but the expression of regret at having to be virtuous.

A girl suffers from violent (psychically), apparently wholly unmotived crying spells. The last one lasted half a day. I inquired whether she had excited herself in some way. Had she any reason for being depressed? No! Was she sure? A trifling matter—" of no particular significance "—occurs to her. On one of the city bridges a very elegant, young gentleman had addressed her. Would she permit him to accompany her? Indignantly she repelled him. What did he think she was! But he persisted in his role; he painted in glowing colours the delights of a rendezvous, till finally she found the courage to exclaim: " If you do not leave me at once, I shall call a policeman! " Then, flushed, bathed in perspiration, she rushed home, ate her meal in silence and soon thereafter gave vent to an almost unending crying spell.

And now I discover that her first attack of crying followed a similar occurrence. She was coming home from the country and had to travel at night. She asked the conductor to point out the ladies' coupé. To her horror a tall, blonde lieutenant entered her coupé at the next station. She at once protested vigorously at the intrusion. The officer very politely offered his apologies, explaining that the train was full and that he would be quite satisfied with a modest corner. He would be greatly obliged to her for her kindness. But so anxious was she about her virtue that she was proof against his entreaties. She appealed to the conductor and insisted on her rights. The spruce officer had to leave the coupé and for the rest of the night she was not molested. But the occurrence had so excited her that she could not fall asleep and she lay awake till dawn. The following day she had the first attack of depression and crying. She bewailed her cruel fate that compelled her to be virtuous while all the hidden voices within clamoured for a gay life. She did not find herself strong enough to conquer her ethical inhibitions. She was too weak to sin and not strong enough to be really virtuous.

I could cite many such examples. They all show convincingly that there are no "inexplicable" psychic depressions, that consciousness does not embrace all the psychic forces that govern and direct us.

The classification of human beings into those that are free and those that are not was determined by a social or ethical canon. But in reality most human beings are the slaves of their unconscious complexes. Only he can be free who knows himself thoroughly, who has dared to look unafraid into the frightful depths of the unconscious. Most persons are under the yoke of their "other self" who, with his biting whip, drives them to pains and to pleasures, compels them to leave the table of life and goads them into the arms of crime.

The greatest happiness in life is to have

achieved one's inner freedom. This thought is still expressed in an old aphorism. "Everyone may have his moods; but his moods must not have him."

Moody persons are the slaves of their past, masters of renunciation and assuredly bunglers in the art of life. Their only salvation is in learning the truth or in the art of transforming their depression into works of art. Most of the time they glide through life's turbulence like dreamers. Their ears are turned inward and thus it comes about that life's call is perceived but faintly by them. They are chasing butterflies in cemeteries. . .

OVERVALUED IDEAS

Ideas resemble coins which have a certain exchange value according to written and unwritten laws. Some are copper coins, so defaced and dirty that no one would suspect from their looks that they had once sparkled like bright gold. Others shine even to-day, after a lapse of a thousand years, and a commanding figure proudly proclaims its origin. One might even more aptly say that ideas resemble securities that are highly valued to-day and may be worthless to-morrow; one day they promise their possessor wealth and fame, and the next day there comes a spiritual break, he is impoverished, and is left with an apparently worthless piece of paper. . .

There is as yet, alas! no standard by which the values of different ideas might be measured. Every man constructs for himself without much ado a canon whereby to value his own thoughts. As a rule he swims with the tide of current opinion; more rarely he goes with the minority and very rarely he independently makes his own measure wherewith to judge matters. Strange! In the end the conflict of minds turns altogether about ideas and their estimation. What else do geniuses, the pathfinders of mankind, accomplish but to disseminate a hitherto neglected or even unknown idea and cause it to be generally accepted or to cause ideas that have hitherto stood high in the world's estimation to topple from their thrones ?

Just as everything else in life runs a circuitous course, in which beginning and end touch, so is it also with the valuation of ideas. Not only the genius, but the fool also strips old, highly esteemed ideas and overvalues others that he has created for himself. The genius and the fool agree in that they permit themselves to be led by the "overvaluation" of their ideas. This expression was coined in a happy moment by the psychiatrist Wernicke. It tells more in its pregnant brevity than a long-winded definition would. Formerly it was the custom to speak of the "fixed ideas" of the sufferers from the peculiar form of insanity which physicians call "paranoia," the mental disease which the laiety knows better and understands less than any other psychosis. A delusion was regarded as a fixed idea which neither experience nor logic could shake. To-day we have penetrated deeper into the problems of delusions. We know that ideas differ from one another tremendously. Some are anemic and colourless, come like pale shadows and so depart. Others have flesh and blood and scintillate in brilliant colours. Long after they have vanished, their image still trembles in our souls in gently dying oscillations. The explanation for this phenomenon is very simple. Our attention is dependent upon our emotions. Pale thoughts are indifferent and have no emphasis. Coloured ideas are richly endowed with emotions, being either pleasurable or painful.

As a rule ideas are in continual conflict with one another. The instincts surge upward from the depth, the inhibitions bear down from above, and between them—owing to stimuli from within and without—the sea of ideas rocks up and down, during which time another idea rises to the mirror-like surface of consciousness. Suddenly one remains on top and becomes stationary, like a buoy anchored deep to the sea's bottom. This is the " fixed idea " of older writers and the " overvalued ideas " of modern psychotherapeutists.

This idea is really deeply anchored. At the bottom of the unconscious lie the great " complexes " which impart a corresponding accent to our various ideas. An overvalued idea is anchored in a " complex " which has repressed all other " complexes." It is accompanied or invested with a powerful affect which has stripped other ideas of their affects.

A very old example—if one may so call it—of physiological insanity is the condition known as " being in love." A German psychiatrist has taken the wholly supererogatory pains to prove anew that a lover is a kind of madman and he designates love as " physiological paranoia." But, unfortunately, he makes no distinction between loving and being in love. But it is just through this distinction that we are enabled precisely to define the conception of an overvalued idea. Like an example from a text-book. For love is an idea whose value is generally acknowledged. We love our parents, our teacher, our country, art, our friends, etc.

But as regards being in love it is quite a different matter. As to this the environment does not accept the exaggerated valuation of the emotions. Here love becomes an overvalued idea. Arguing with one who is in love about common sense, religion, education, station, or politics will not affect him in the least. He is dominated solely by the love-complex. This alone determines the resonance of his thoughts and feelings. The attraction to the chosen object has attracted all the other affects to it, has placed all the impulses at the service of one overvalued idea. He loves life but only if he be together with his beloved; he is jealous, but only with reference to the love-object; he is interested only in such matters as are in some way related to that object. The fool who is being dominated by an overvalued idea acts exactly in the same way. The lunatic who imagines himself the king of the world, and in whom a childhood wish had overpoweringly established itself as a fact in his consciousness, has interest only for such things as find access to this wish; the victim of ideas of persecution discovers in the news items of the daily papers the important communication that his enemies are laying traps for him; the unfortunate love-sick youth who imagines that Princess X wants to give him her hand in marriage sees in all sorts of advertisements of love-hungry ladies secret communications from his princess.

These poor fools bring everything they see and everything they feel into relationship with the overvalued idea which, projected outward in the shape of an hallucination, sounds to their ears like a spiritual echo and blinds their eyes like a vision.

A lover acts essentially like this. That is why the world says of a person in love that he makes himself ridiculous. A handkerchief or a glove, or anything belonging to the beloved, becomes a fetich which can evoke the most ecstatic emotions. Anything that can be associated with love is overvalued.

Another question involuntarily presents itself. Is love, in the form known as " being in love," the only overvalued idea with which a normal person may be afflicted? Are there any other forms of " physiological insanity "—if we may use the term coined by Lower and subsequently imitated by Moebius?

The answer to these questions is not difficult. A backward look teaches us what unspeakable evils overvalued ideas have wrought in man's history. For overvalued ideas are sources of great danger. They are richly endowed with emotions and consequently lend themselves to suggestion more readily than almost any other idea. Bleuler has proved that suggestion is nothing but the transference of an emotion. And such overvalued ideas can be hurled with great suggestive force among the multitude and change the individual—and even whole communities—into a fool. That is how the psychoses of whole nations have arisen. The tremendous power of overvalued ideas can be understood if one thinks of the crusades, the witchcraft persecutions, hysterical epidemics, the Dreyfus affair, anarchism, etc.

It is a sad fact that none of us can be free from overvalued ideas. In this sense there is really no difference between fools and healthy persons. Everyone of us bears within himself a hidden quantity of neurosis and psychosis. What saves us from the insane asylum is perhaps only the circumstance that we hide our overvalued ideas or that so many persons share our folly and that the multitude accepts it as wisdom.

There are innumerable aphorisms, the crystallised precipitations of thousands of years, experience, that express this truth. " Every man has his little crack, his dross and his sliver." (In the German saying the overvalued idea is compared to a splinter in the brain. An excellent mataphor !) " If you see a fool take hold of your own ears." " You cannot name a wise man who was not guilty of some folly." (The reader will find ample material on this subject in Dr. Moenkenmöller's book on ' mental disease and mental weakness in satire, proverb, and humour,' published in 1907.) In other words : We all suffer from a false and subjective valuation of our ideas. We all drag overvalued ideas about with us.

It is the dream of all great minds to revise these overvalued ideas. Nietzsche's life work was a struggle with overvalued ideas. While so engaged, he himself became the victim of an overvalued idea, and his superman will forever remain a literary myth. But if the twilight of Gods could once set in for the overvalued ideas then only could we do full justice to his rhapsodies in "Beyond Good and Evil." For in no other sphere is there such luxuriance of overvalued ideas as in the ethical. All progress has been brought about by the suppression of the natural impulses. All our education, using the word in its true sense, consists in investing our instincts and impulses with dont's. The sum total of these inhibitions we call morality. Progress consists in getting pleasure out of the inhibition, in converting the displeasure of being inhibited into ethical pleasure. The striving for this goal results in a kind of ethical burdening. One who has had the opportunity to study neurotics will be amazed at the many agonizing conscious pangs they suffer from owing to their ignorance of man's true nature. These times pant under the burden of morality as an overvalued idea. They are in danger of asphyxiating under the ethical burden. A false and hypocritical morality, by disseminating an unhealthy conception of our dispositions (instincts), has turned our views on what constitutes sin topsy-turvy. The consequences are only too evident. On the one hand, we behold, as evidences of suppression, indulgence in frivolities, pleasure in the piquant, a delight in indelicate jokes, which forcibly intrude into life and art; on the other hand, as the natural reaction to this, an over-luxuriance of scientific and pseudo-scientific sexual literature. And all because morality became a ruinously overvalued idea. I do not wish to be misunderstood. Morality will always remain the goal of noble souls, but only that kind of morality which harmonizes with man's nature. Where morality does violence to nature it becomes natural, and brings about not ethical freedom but ethical burdening.

But morality is not the only overvalued idea that turns the half of mankind into fools. If we survey the chaos of modern social life we shall easily find everywhere evidences of the endless disputes and irritating conflicts caused by overvalued ideas. Scientists may prove that the theory of races is no longer tenable, that the asserted purity of races is a fable, etc. Notwithstanding all that, the German Workurka and the Checko rustic are always at each other's throats. Why cite other examples? In racial, religious, national, and other discords it is always an overvalued idea that makes a harmonious evolution impossible. Verily, the whole world is an insane asylum because the essential factor in delusions, an overvalued idea, pervades the air like infectious psychic germs.

Will the world ever be better? From a

survey of the past we are justified only in being coldly sceptical and discouragingly dubious. A conflict of ideas will continue as long as there are dissensions between human beings. Ideas to wage a war for exsistence. A few survive longer than others, are highly esteemed till their course is run and are discovered to have been overvalued. But as long as they have the mastery they change credulous men into foolish children.

From this endless round there is no escape. And folly and wisdom lead the never-ending dance until the dark, wide open gates of the future swallow them.

AFFECTIONATE PARENTS

The last few years the child has become the centre of interest. Funny as it may sound, it may almost be asserted that we had just rediscovered the child. Congresses are held, artists devote their talents to portraying the life of the child, expositions acquaint us with the many aspects of the advances that have been made in the new knowledge. Is it any wonder then that we have suddenly been made acquainted with the abuses of children? That we have shudderingly learned that there are children who are tortured by their own mothers? There were loud cries of horror. The fountain of humanity became a broad stream which must drive the mills of a new social organization in the interests of the defenceless child. Who would withhold his approval of this movement? Who would oppose it? For truly there is no sadder spectacle than a child tortured to death by its own parents. The whole instinct for race preservation cries out against it. . .

But this theme may also be regarded from another angle, and I purpose showing from the point of view of the physician and the pedagog that the reverse of abuse, viz., excessive affection, has a dark side, that it, too, is capable of ruining a child's life and condemning an innocent being to lifelong suffering.

At a private gathering of physicians not long ago the subject of the last congress for the protection of children was discussed from its more serious as well as lighter aspects. A Viennese neurologist ventured the following remark: "I regard it as a great misfortune if a woman's affection for her husband is expended upon her child. A misfortune for humanity, for, in this way, the number of nervous persons will be incalculably increased."

One is strongly inclined at first energetically to attack this opinion. What! A tender, affectionate bringing up will make a child neurotic? Who can prove that a happy childhood results in an unhappy life? Shall parents be afraid to show their children love? To hug them, kiss them, pet them? Is not nervousness rather the sequel to draconic sternness, tyrannical compulsion?

Nonsense! Nonsense! I shall attempt to answer these obtrusive questions seriatim.

But, first, one remarkable fact has to be postulated. Parents are really becoming more and more affectionate from year to year. Such fanatically affectionate parents as are quite common now were formerly the exception. Today the parents' thoughts all centre around the child: How to feed it, bring it up, dress it hygienically, harden it, how to instruct it in sexual matters. . . . A flood of books and magazines scarcely suffices to meet the tremendous concern about these matters. Can this emanate solely from the fact that the pressing movement for emancipation of woman has displaced the woman's interest from the man to the child ? I think that herein the neurologist is in error. That cannot possibly be the sole cause.

The cause for the hypertrophied love of the child is adduced from the consideration of those cases which even in former times offered instances of an exaggerated parental affection amounting to doting love. The over-indulged child was almost invariably an only child whom popular speech designates a " trembling joy."

It is to be regretted that most modern families are made up of such " trembling joys." " Neo-Malthusianism " has infected the whole world. In consequence of the employment of innumerable and more or less generally employed anti-conceptives the birth rate is steadily declining. " Two-children families " is the rule, and families with many children—especially among the well-to-do—the exception. Even the vaunted fecundity of the Germans which is always being held up as a model to the French will soon be a thing of the past. In former decades 1,000 married women in Berlin gave birth to 220 children and from 1873 to 1877 the number even rose to 231. Since then the birth rate is declining from year to year, so that in 1907 1,000 women only had 111 children. In other large cities matters are even worse than in Berlin in this regard. But it would be decidedly wrong to infer that there is a diminution in the number of marriages. In Prussia the number of marriages from 1901 to 1904 was at the rate of 8 per 1,000, whereas in 1850 it was somewhat less, to wit: 7·8 per 1,000. Sociologists have detected in this state of affairs a great danger for the mental prospects of the race inasmuch as matters in this regard are much better in the country and, consequently, they say, the progeny of the farmer class will in a not remote period tremendously exceed the intelligent descendants of urban people in number. The country will get the best of the city and not vice versa. But we must not wander away from our subject. Let us take this fact for granted: The "two-children system" is the cause for the excessive parental affection we have described. But wherein is this dangerous?

I shall not attempt here a detailed statement of the well-known dangers. We all know that coddled children very often become helpless, dependent persons, that they cannot find their place in life, and do not seem to be armed against adversity. It seems superfluous to dwell at greater length on this. Of greater significance is the phenomenon that the exaggerated affection lavished on the child creates a correspondingly large need for affection in it. A need for affection that is tempestuous in its demand for gratification. As long as these children are young so long is this demand fully satisfied. The parents, and especially mothers, are so overjoyed at their children's manifestations of love that out of their overflowing hearts they reward them by overwhelming them with caresses. Thus the measure of affectionate demonstrations rises instead of gradually sinking. And now the time comes for the child to go to school. And for the first time in its life it stands in the presence of the will of a stranger who demands neither petting nor love, only work done without grumbling. How easily this situation gives rise to conflict! The child thinks it is not loved by the teacher, it is terrified by a harsh word and begins to cry. School becomes odious to it; it learns unwillingly. It asks for another school and for other teachers. If its wish is gratified the same thing is soon repeated.

Matters get much worse when these children grow up. They have an unquenchable craving for caresses. From them are developed the women who kill their husband's love by their own immoderate love. Every day they want to be told that their husbands still love them. Daily—nay, hourly—they wish to be the recipients of sweets, loving words, private pet names and kisses without number. The men, on the other hand, who had been so coddled in their childhood, are only in the rarest instances satisfied with their wives; sooner or later they seek to compensate outside of the home for the insufficient affection shown by the wife; or they transfer this requirement upon the children who thus become seriously (though not congenitally) burdened. But even this is not the worst.

The greatest dangers of excessive affection are known to only very few persons. They consist in a premature excitation of the erotic emotions. We are so prone to forget unpleasant experiences. Hence comes it that most adults have no recollection of their own youthful erotic experiences. Parents especially are very forgetful in this regard—so much so that their forgetfulness amounts almost to a pathological condition bordering on hysterical amnesia. Thence comes it that most mothers will take an oath on their daughters' innocence and fathers on their sons' purity. They talk themselves into the belief that their children are exceptions, that they are incredibly simple, still believe in the stork myth and other similar stupidities.

That the sexual enlightenment of the child is an important problem and of far-reaching significance for its whole life is proved in numberless books and essays dealing with the subject. We are told that open scientific instruction should take the place of secret knowledge obtained from turbid channels. Very fine! But the world must not believe that the child's first erotic knowledge is awakened as a result of such instruction. That is a widespread superstition. The sexual life of the child does not begin with puberty, the old books to the contrary notwithstanding, but with the day of its birth.

On the occasion of a sad criminal trial in

which children were charged with being prostitutes, public opinion was horrified at the wickedness of these poor creatures. And yet most of them were victims of their environment. Does any one really believe that such occurrences are rare exceptions? That is a myth. We talk ourselves into the belief that the little child that is still unable to speak is not receptive to erotic impressions. How do we know this? The brain of a child is like a photographic plate that greedily catches impressions, independently of whether they are intelligible or not, impressions whose influence may be operative throughout its life. As we know, there is a large group of investigators which traces all perverse manifestations of the sexual impulses back to a fixation of the earliest erotic experience. Erotic stimulation can subsequently be brought about only by way of an association with this early impression. This explanation certainly does seem to fit the curious phenomenon known as fetichism. In this way children's experiences influence their whole life. In sexual matters human beings behave with incredible naiveté. They close their eyes and will not see. Frank Wedekind is perfectly right in deriding a world that has secrets even from itself. So infantile sexuality is a secret which every intelligent person knows.

If parents only kept this in their mind's eye! Then it would not happen that children ten years of age and older would be permitted to sleep in their parents' bedrooms that the anxious father and mother might watch over the gentlest breath of their precious darlings. These parents do not want to consider the possibility that the children may in this way receive impressions which may prove very injurious to them. Many a case of obstinate insomnia in childhood or of nocturnal attacks of apprehension is explained in this way. I have repeatedly cured sleepless children by the simple remedy of ordering them to sleep in separate bedrooms.

Let us assume then that all children are susceptible to erotic stimuli and that such stimulation may harm them. For the later a person's conscious sexual life begins the greater the prospects of his becoming a healthy, mentally well-balanced individual. Among the factors capable of permanently arousing erotic emotions we must include excessive affection. Between the affections of one who loves and of a mother there are really no differences. Both kiss, caress, fondle, hug, embrace, pet, etc. That the excitement is transmitted to the same central organs is obvious.

In this way the child receives its first erotic sensations from its nurse. Interpret it as we may the nurse, the attendant, the mother, the father are the child's first love, the first erotic love, as our psychoanalysis has convincingly demonstrated. But this must not be interpreted to mean that I wish to condemn the affectionate management of children. On the contrary!

A certain quantity of affection is, as a matter of fact, essential to the normal development of the individual. But the affection lavished on them must not be excessive. For if it is the child will be prematurely brought into a condition of erotic overstimulation. It grows older and begins to feel the power of education. To restrain and curb the force of the natural impulses powerful inhibitions are erected. As a reaction to the premature sexual stimulation there begins a remarkable process which may be designated as "sexual repression." This repression may succeed so well that even the child forgets its early experiences or the repression does not succeed and the individual's erotic requirements grow from year to year. In the latter case there develops in the child a serious psychic conflict between sexual longing and sexual renunciation and thus the soil in which a neurosis may grow is prepared. Perhaps the conflict is the neurosis.

We shall mention only in passing that such exaggerated affection begets in many children the habit of securing for themselves a certain amount of pleasurable sensations by way of certain auto-erotic actions. It is not possible, nor necessary, to enter into a detailed discussion of these matters here. For most people know that our experiences in childhood influence our whole life. But it is a tragic commentary on human strivings that excessive parental love may bring sickness upon the child, that a happy present is replaced by an unhappy future, that the roses a mother strews in her child's path only later show their thorns.

We cannot say it too often : We fuss too much with our children. There is too much theory in this matter of bringing up children. We pay too much attention to our children. Let us leave them their peaceful childhood, their merry games, the wondrous product of their untiring phantasy. Let us clearly realize that with our excessive affection we give ourselves a great deal of pleasure but that at the same time we are doing the children a great injury. Let no one discourage mothers from being affectionate to their children, from expending loving attentions on them, from making their youth as pleasant as possible. But the parents' affection should not expend itself mechanically. It should be a uniformly warm fire that only warms, kindles no fire, and bursts into a bright flame only on life's great holidays.

WHY THEY QUARREL

When a happy married couple laughingly assures me that the heaven of their marriage was always cloudless and that there were no thunderstorms and no lightning flashes I accept it as self-evident, but to myself I think: they are lying. When two friends assure me that they have never quarrelled I think the same thing. I know that they have not been telling the truth. That is, they are liars without the consciousness of lying. They are firmly convinced that they were telling only what was true, because they have "repressed" the unpleasant, the painful, the objectionable. And thus it comes to pass that lovers forget all the "scenes" that had occurred between them, and that friends become oblivious of the little unpleasantnesses that had caused them so much suffering, and that they can assert, with the utmost conviction, that they had never quarrelled. We do not quaff the lethe-potion of oblivion at our life's end. No, we sip it daily, and it is this that enables us to maintain that optimism which ever looks hopefully into the future and anticipates thornless roses.

There are people who must always be quarrelling, whose exuberant energy must be discharged in this way, to whom life does not seem worth while if it runs along smoothly. These are the everlastingly unsatisfied who have not found the ideals of their youth, who have not attained their dreams. They project their discontent, their internal distraction, upon all their daily experiences. That is why they so often appear to be overcharged with emotion ; that is why the intensity of their excitement is imcomprehensible to us. For it is a fact that they fly into rages about trivial matters. But it is this very intensity of emotion that shows that there is more behind these little rows than they will ordinarily admit, that the quarrel derives its fuel from a deeper source than appears on the surface.

It has struck many observers that the external provocation to quarrelling is often very trivial. Of course we frequently hear a man or his wife declare that they would gladly avoid a quarrel if it were possible to do so. Either one says something that seems to be quite innocent, and yet it will be the occasion for a heated altercation, a great domestic scene with all its unpleasant consequences.

This is due to the fact that most persons do not distinguish between cause and provocation. The provocation to a quarrel is easily found if hidden unconscious forces seek for it, if a deeper cause, acting as a driving power, sets the wheels of passion in motion.

A somewhat careful investigation of every quarrel easily brings the conviction that it is invariably the secret, unconscious emotions that bring about the conflict of opinions. Where this deep resonance of the unconscious is lacking we playfully pass over differences. Unfortunately there are probably no two human beings whose souls vibrate so harmoniously that there never occurs a discord. This phenomenon is altogether too deeply rooted in human nature for an exception ever to occur. And paradoxical as it may sound, it is lovers who love each other most who cause each other the greatest pain. The great intensity which their emotions attain is due only to the fact they have repressed a series of experiences and feelings. They are blind to the faults of the beloved because they do not wish to see these faults. But the suppressed forces have not yet lost their power over the soul. These bring about the quarrel, and are capable, even if only for a few seconds, to transform love into hatred.

But a few practical examples will do more to make this subject clear than all our theoretical explanations. Mr. N. S., a pious, upright man, asserts that his present ailment dates from a quarrel that had been frightfully upsetting him for months. He had inherited from his father a large library rich in manuscripts, and had also succeeded him in his position. One day his brother came to him and stormily demanded the return of the books. But inasmuch as he was the older he felt himself entitled to be the sole heir. A violent quarrel ensued, during which he exclaimed: "I'll die before I give up any of these books!" After the quarrel he became very neurotic. He tortures himself with self-reproaches; he is convinced that with that exclamation he had been guilty of an act of impiety; he is very unhappy and finds no rest, no peace, either at home or in his office.

Many persons may be satisfied with the superficial explanation offered by the patient himself that he is an ardent bibliophile and collector of ancient manuscripts. But the physician who treats sick souls must not be so easily satisfied.

We know that every collector is an unconscious Don Juan who has transferred his passion from an erotic upon a non-erotic sphere. But we also know that the passion with which the collected objects are loved emanates from the erotic domain. And what did our psychoanalysis of the above case bring out? Remarkably enough a rivalry between the two brothers which went back all the way to their youth. The older one had the privileges of the first-born and was a good-for-nothing. The younger one was a pattern of what a child ought to be. From their childhood they had been rivals for the affection of their parents, and more especially of the mother. We encounter here the so-called "Oedipus motive," a son's love for his mother—a motive whose instinctive force and urge are still too imperfectly appreciated. The two had been rivals, the older one being jealous of the parents' preference for the younger one, and the younger jealous of the older one's privileges. In this we have the first of the deeper motives for the quarrel. Further investigation brought a second and a third motive to light. The older had, very naturally, married first, and repeatedly boasted in the presence of his younger and unmarried brother of his wife's charms and virtues. In fact, he had even led him into his wife's bedroom that he might see for himself what a treasure he possessed. (You see the motives of such stories as "Gyges and his Ring" and "King Candaules" occurring even nowadays.) At that moment a great passion for his sister-in-law flared up in the younger brother's breast. Here we have then a second cause for dissension. But other factors are also involved. Our pious young man married a beautiful woman and would have been happy if he had not been the victim of a jealous passion. Jealousy always has its origin in the knowledge of one's inferiority. He thought he noticed that his older brother was too devoted to his wife. And during an excursion into the country they had been in the woods a little too long, as he thought, and it occurred to him—and here we have the fourth motive—to tempt his sister-in-law. He is a Don Juan who runs after every petticoat and wants to drain life in large draughts. N. S. was a pious virtuous man who knew how to turn his sinful cravings to good account for the success of his business and to bad account as far as his health was concerned. The brother whom he despised openly he envied in secret. But we could mention still other motives for their quarrel if Mrs. Grundy considerations did not bar the way . . .

Unconscious sexual motives lurk behind many quarrels, one might almost say behind most quarrels. We have already hinted that dissensions between brothers or sisters are due to rivalry. But even in the quarrels between parents and children we may frequently enough demonstrate the identical undertone for the disharmony. The infant son sees in his father a rival for the mother's favour. The reverse also occurs, though not so frequently. I was once the witness to a violent quarrel between a father and his son. The father had, as it seemed to me, not the slightest cause for grievance against the son, and yet a little trifle led to a violent altercation that ended in a tragic scene. At the height of the row the father screamed to his wife: "You are to blame for it all! You robbed me of my son's love!"

Naturally one would think that this lava stream belched forth in a great burst of passion from a volcano would contain the truth in its torrid current. And so it does, but in a disguised form. The true reproach should have been directed at the son, and should have been: "You have robbed me of my wife's love!"

We see in this a "transference" of a painful emotion from one person upon another. Such transferences or "displacements" are extremely common in everyday life, and it is only with their aid that we can account for the many domestic conflicts. A man will rarely admit that he erred in the choice of a wife. The feeling of hatred that his wife engenders in him he transfers upon others. Upon whom? The answer is obvious. Upon her next of kin. Most frequently upon her mother, the most immediate cause of her existence. This is the secret meaning of the many mother-in-law jokes, a never-failing and inexhaustible and perpetual theme for wits.

So that, for example, if we hear a young woman complain that she cannot bear her husband's family but that she loves him beyond bounds we may with perfect safety translate this in the language of the unconscious thus: "I would not care a rap about my husband's family if I did not have to love my husband."

The rows with servants, well-known daily occurrences, become intelligible only if we know the law of transference. An unfaithful wife, who had been betrayed and deserted by her lover, suddenly began to watch her servant girls suspiciously, and to strike them on the slightest provocations. The woman had for years employed "help" without having had more than the customary quarrels with them. After a short sojourn with her husband the rage of the abandoned woman, who would have loved to give her faithless lover a good thrashing in true southern fashion, was transferred upon her servants. And exactly like this the resentment of many a housewife is discharged through these more or less innocent lightning rods, and thus is brought about the phenomenon so common in modern large cities which may be designated as "servant-girl neurosis."

Obviously the deeper motives slumber in the unconscious, and if they ever become conscious they are looked upon as sinfulness and bad temper. Freud has become the founder of a wholly new psychology by virtue of his discovery of the laws of repression and of transference—a psychology which will be indispensable to the criminologist of the future. What is nowadays brought to light in our halls of justice as the psychological bases for conflicts is generally only superficial psychology.

This is strikingly illustrated by one of the saddest of legal proceedings of last year. I mean the trial for murder in the Murri-Boumartini case, in consequence of which an innocent victim—so I am convinced—the Countess Linda Boumartini is languishing in prison. Her brother Tullio, who had murdered his brother-in-law, was accused of an illicit relationship with his sister, for otherwise the murder would have been inexplicable. One who has carefully read Linda's memoirs and her letters, which are now before the public, as well as the confessions of the imprisoned Tullio, will be sure to laugh at the accusation, which unquestionably owed its origin to a clerical plot. What may have really happened is that unconscious brotherly love which deep down under consciousness in all likelihood takes it origin from the sexual but whose flowers appear on the surface of consciousness as the loftiest manifestations of ethical feeling. It was brotherly love, the primal motive which Wagner immortalised in his "Walkyre," that forced the dagger into Tullio Murri's hand. He saw his sister suffer and go to pieces because of the brutal stupidity of his brother-in-law. What lay hidden behind his pure fraternal love may never have entered his consciousness.

Oh, we unfortunates, doomed to eternal blindness! What we see of the motives of great conflicts is usually only the surface. Even in the case of the little domestic quarrels, the irritating frictions of everyday life, the vessel of knowledge sails only over the easily excited ripples. But what gives these waters their black aspect is the deep bed over which they lie. Down there, at the bottom of the sea which represents our soul, there ever abide ugly, deformed monsters—our instincts and desires—emanating from the beginnings of man's history. When they bestir their coarse bodies the sea too trembles and is slightly set in motion. And we stupid human beings think it is the surface wind that has begot the waves.

LOOKING INTO THE FUTURE

It was getting late. The last guests had left the café. The waiters, tired and sleepy, were prowling around our table with a peculiar expression in their countenances which clearly challenged us to call for our checks . . .

We took no notice of them. Or rather, we refused to take notice. The sudden death of one of our dearest friends had aroused something incomprehensible in us which made us very restless. We were speaking about premonitions, and that peculiar intangible awe which one feels in the presence of the incomprehensible, the supernatural, which at certain times overcomes even the most confirmed sceptic, sat at our table.

The journalist—who could not deny a slight tendency to mysticism—was of the opinion that he would certainly not die a natural death. That was all we could get him to say on the subject at this time. Finally however he confessed, with pretended indifference, that he has the certain premonition that he will one day be trampled to death by frightened horses.

" Nonsense ! "—" Nursery tales ! "—" Superstition ! " several voices exclaimed simultaneously

But the physician shook his head gravely.

"Strange! Very strange! Do you put any stock in this looking into the future?"

The journalist blushed so slightly that it could hardly be noticed, the way men blush when they fear that they had betrayed a weakness. Cautiously he replied: "And why not? Can you prove the contrary? Have we not until only a few years ago pooh-poohed the idea of telepathy and called it superstition? But now-a-days that the X-rays, wireless telegraphy and other marvels have revolutionised our ideas about matter and energy and even space, we no longer laugh pityingly at the poor dreamers who, like Swedenburg, the northern magician, see things that are beyond the field of vision of their bodily eyes. Why then should I doubt the possibility of somebody some day finding an explanation for the ability to 'look into the future'?"

"Bosh!" exclaimed the lawyer. "That's all fantastic piffle! I can cite you an example from my own experience which is as interesting as it is instructive. I was very sick and confined to bed. Suddenly I awoke, my heart palpitating, and heard a loud voice screaming these words right into my ears: 'You will live fourteen days more! Take advantage of this period!' Just fourteen days later I was sailing on the ocean. A frightful sirocco wind was tossing our little steamer from right to left and from left to right so violently that we could not retain our upright positions. And suddenly my prophecy—which I had almost completely forgotten—came back to me. But I remained very cool, like a scientist who is on the eve of making a great discovery and risking his life to do so. As you see I did not die, and the ship came safely into port. But had I accidentally perished, and if my prophetic dream—the outward projection of my unconscious fear—my unpleasant hallucination had been known to the people about me—the matter would have been construed as a new confirmation of the truth of premonitions. We have so many premonitions that are never fulfilled that the few that happen accidentally to come true do not really matter. Lots of things in life are that way. We speak of our 'hard luck' because we forget the times when we have been lucky. Luck rushes by so swiftly! Bad luck creeps, oh, so slowly! And, coming down to facts, I do not know of a single instance of an undoubted fulfillment of a prophecy. For I must confess that all these American and Berlin prophets who have recently given such striking proofs of their 'second sight' do not impress me. They have not uttered a single prophecy precisely and accurately, and oracular speeches delivered in general terms are as elastic as a rubber band, and can be applied to almost anything. A great conflagration, a destructive earthquake, or a cruel war will rarely disappoint a prophet. Somewhere or other in this wide world there is a conflagration some time during the year, the earth rocks somewhere, and somewhere machine guns are being fired. I therefore do not believe that our friend will be trampled to death by frightened horses. At the most what will happen will be that his pegasus, growing tired of being abused by him, will suddenly throw him down."

For a little while there was silence. We had the feeling that the counsellor's malicious witti-ism was out of place at this time. The doctor broke the silence. "What will you say, my dear friends, if I tell you that a prominent scientist and psychologist has reported a case which seems to prove the possibility of looking into the future. I say 'seems' only because there is an explanation which re-transforms the supernatural into the natural. The physician in question, the well-known Dr. Flournoy, had frequently been consulted by a young man who was suffering from peculiar attacks of apprehension. Day and night he was haunted by the idea that he would fall from a high mountain into a deep precipice, and so be killed. Logic and persuasion were of no avail in dealing with this obsession. It was easy enough for Flournoy to point out that all the young man had to do was to keep away from mountains, and there would be no possibility of his meeting such a frightful end. The patient grew very melancholic, and could not be persuaded to enjoy life as formerly. Imagine this experienced psychologist's amazement on reading in his newspaper one day that his patient had been instantly killed by accidentally falling from a steep but easily passable ridge while he was taking a walk in a sanitarium in the Alps."

The journalist exclaimed triumphantly: "Doctor, you've disproved your own theory. If what you've just told us doesn't prove the power to look into the future, then nothing does."

"Pish! Pish!" replied the physician. "Haven't I said that the explanation is to follow?"

We were all very curious to hear how such a strange occurrence could be explained without the aid of the supernatural. The physician lit another cigar and continued: "What, coming down to facts, is fear? You all know what it is, for I have told you often enough: fear—anxiety—apprehension—is a repressed wish. Every time that two wishes are in conflict as to which one is to have mastery over the individual the wish that has to yield is perceived in consciousness as apprehension. A young girl is apprehensive when she finds herself for the first time alone in a room with her sweetheart. For the time being she is afraid of what later on she may wish for. Dr. Flournoy's melancholic young man was clearly tired of life. The wish may have come upon him once to make an end of his life by throwing himself from a great height—from such a height as would make failure of the suicidal attempt impossible. This wish may have come to him at night in a dream, or perhaps just before he fell asleep, while he was in a state between sleep and waking. Who knows? But it must have prevailed before the will to live had repressed it and converted it into apprehension. And his prophetic premonitions were nothing but the misunderstood voice from within. And his mysterious death was nothing but—suicide. I have forgotten to tell you that, according to the newspaper reporters, he had sat down on the edge of a precipice and fallen asleep. He had fallen down while asleep. As if the voices in his dream had whispered to him: 'Come! do what you so earnestly yearn to do! Die! Now you have a fine opportunity!' The moment had come when the fear had become the stronger wish."

The journalist was pale. The doctor's explanation seemed to have stirred up something in the deepest layers of his soul. His voice box was seen to make that automatic movement which we all make when we are embarrassed, as if we wished to speak but could not find the right word. Finally, after he had coughed a little several times, as if to clear his vocal cords, he remarked in a somewhat heavy voice: "That would throw a peculiar light upon many accidental falls in the mountains. You recall, no doubt, that a short time ago a well-known tourist had fallen from a relatively safe cliff. He carried a lot of insurance, and the insurance companies were very anxious to prove it a case of suicide. Is it possible that in this case, too, an "unconscious power co-operated?"

"Certainly!" exclaimed the physician. "Certainly! At any rate, it is my conviction that many persons seek nothing but death in the mountains. I have certainly met many tourists who had nothing more to hope for from life. One who does not fear death no longer loves life, or, at any rate, no longer loves it to such an extent as not to be willing to gamble with it. Have any of you an idea how many of our actions have their origin in 'unconscious' motives? All our life our shadow, our other self, walks by our side and has its say in everything we do. As long as it is only a shadow it is not dangerous. But, woe, if the shadow materialises, as the spiritualists say. The tourist makes a false step and falls into an abyss. Who or what guided his foot? Was it chance—or the unacted wish that slumbered so long beyond the threshold of consciousness? Or shall we say that while one was climbing up a steep mountain path his strength failed him, and he was precipitated into the depths below? Who can decide in such a case as to just what happened? For a little moment the climber must have had the thought 'if you are not careful now you will fall and be killed.' The next moment there may have issued from the repressed 'complexes' the command: 'Do it! Then you are free and rid of all your troubles!' So our young man could have continued to live on the even ground, as Flournoy had advised him to do. But he preferred to go to the mountains. Perhaps it would be better to say that something drew him to the mountains. It was the same power that precipitated him into the abyss: his life-weariness. The trip he took to the country for the sake of his health was from the very beginning a flight into the realm of death. He pursued his shadow just as———"

He did not finish his sentence. His cigar had gone out. He lit it again, and with wide open eyes gazed into the distance as if he had more to say but could not find the right word.

There was silence for a time, and finally the counsellor ventured to say: "Very interesting case! I wonder if its psychology could not be generalised? Isn't it possible that a large number of the other daily fatal accidents could not be instances of 'unconscious suicide'? There is, for example, the case of the man who is run over by a cable-car because he did not hear the bell, the unlucky swimmer who is overcome by cramps, the victim of the fellow who did not know the revolver was loaded. Haven't all these little and big accidents their shadowy motivation?"

"Of course they have," replied the physician. "Of course! We really know so little of the things we do and even less why we do them. Our emotions, our feelings, are really only the resultants of numerous components; they are only tensions giving shadowy testimony of ripening forces. We think we are directing these forces, but we are being driven by them; we think we make our decisions, but we only accept the decisions of 'the other fellow' in us.

Professor Freud has assured himself a place amongst the immortals with his psychological theory concerning so-called 'symptomatic acts.' He has substituted a 'secret inner will' for 'blind chance.'"

"And what about looking into the future?" inquired the journalist.

"Why, that's only looking backward. We can easily predict for ourselves anything we long for, and can easily have presentiments about what we do not wish to avert. The facts which permit us to glimpse the future are gleaned from our yesterdays. Our childhood wishes determine our subsequent history. All of us could readily read our future could we call into new life our childhood emotions. What we dreamed of in childhood we wish to experience as adults. And if we cannot experience it we are drawn back into the realm of eternal dreams. This is as true of humanity as a whole as of man individually. Only when we study our past can we see the future of our present, then can we predict that our modern, ultra-modern time with its innumerable stupidities, with its conflicts and ideals, with its strivings and discoveries, will be as far outstripped as we imagine ourselves to have outstripped our ancestors. Science and art, politics and public life—all a perpetual circle tending towards an unknown future. . ."

"So then, to return to my glimpse of the future," the journalist interrupted, "that I shall be crushed by runaway horses?"

The physician smiled superiorly. " Just try to think back and see whether your presentiment has not its roots in the past ! "

" Something now occurs to me," exclaimed the mystic ; " my mother used to prophesy that I would not die a natural death. I was a very wild youth, and managed to spend a lot of time with the horses in our stable. In great anger my dear little mother would then launch all sorts of gloomy predictions concerning my destiny."

His mysterious look into the future was now explained. The doctor ventured to remark that this " case " also illustrated how intimately superstition and a consciousness of guilt are linked together. The imaginary glimpse into the future was in his friend's case also only a glimmer out of the past. He referred to the remarkable fact that our earliest recollections represent a reflection of our future. . . .

" There are facts "—he said slowly, hesitatingly, as if the words had to be forced out of his interior—" which one can hardly explain. I once loved a woman with such an intense love as I have not felt for any woman since. We spent a wonderful day together. Then we bade each other good-night. I remained standing, looking after her. She was walking through the high reeds in a meadow. Her graceful figure was getting smaller and smaller. With a slight turn in the road she disappeared from my view but soon reappeared. Then for a while I saw her shadowy outline until a clump of trees again hid her from my view. Then I saw her again, but very small. I saw something white—her handkerchief. At this moment a shiver went through me, and I thought: that's how you will lose her; gradually you will cease to see her; twice she will re-appear, and then she will be gone for ever!—Nonsense, said I to myself, and spun bold plans for the future. . . . But the future proved that my presentiment had been true. Everything happened as I had felt it that evening. A glimpse into the future! And yet! Sometimes I think to myself that I had only realised the impossibility of a union between us. What I felt as a presentiment may have been only clearer inner comprehension."

The waiter yawned loud. This time we took the hint and paid. We went home, and something oppressive, unspoken, weighed us all down. As if we were not quite satisfied with the solution of the mystery—as if the shuddering sweetness of a superstitious belief in supernatural powers, a belief in a something above and beyond us would be more to our liking. Silently we took our way through the quiet streets. We felt, for all the world, like children who had been told by their mother that the beautiful story was only a story—that the prince and the princess had never really lived.

We had been robbed of one of life's fairy tales. Fie! Fie on this naked, sober, empty reality! How much nicer it would be if we could look into the future!

LOOKING BACKWARD

Around Christmas of every year a pale woman clad in black consults me and bewails her fate. It is a pitiful tale that she narrates tearfully. A ruined life, a ruined marriage! One of those fearful disappointments experienced by women who, utterly unacquainted with the world, and not brought up to be independent, entrust all their dammed-up longing for happiness and love to the first man who happens to cross their path. The first time she came I was touched with pity and could have wept with her. The best advice I could give her was wholly to separate from her husband, forget the past, and to build up a new life. The second time she came I was somewhat unpleasantly surprised, because the unfortunate woman had not yet screwed her courage to the sticking-point and was wasting her life in gloomy broodings about the incomprehensibleness of her destiny. But this time she promised to employ all the means and resources at her disposal to get out of her fruitless conflict and useless complainings. . . . Since her first visit ten years have passed, but she still stands on the ruins of her hopes and laments her wasted life. Her figure, which was once slender and sinewy, looks as if it were broken in many parts; her face shows the first traces of age. Now she has additional cause for grieving. She looks into the mirror and is unhappy that she has changed so. " What has become of me and the beauty that so many admired ? " Before her mind's eye she sees again the men who once wooed her and whom she had rejected. Every one of them would probably have made her happier than the one she had chosen !

She augments her complainings and emphasizes her despair. All her friends and all her relatives, her physicians and her confidants, know her sad lot and have no new words of consolation for her, only conventional phrases and stereotyped gestures. Because of her complainings she is becoming a nuisance to everybody. Her pain has reached that dangerous point where the tragic becomes the comic. In vain she tries to move her hearers by heightening the dramatic description of the unalterableness of her situation. She becomes aware that human beings can become partisans only in the presence of fresh conflicts and very quickly become accustomed to others' unhappiness. And this, of course, gives her additional reason for thinking herself lonesome, misunderstood, and forsaken, and thus a new melody is added to her stale song. If she had before this compared herself with her happier sisters, her consciousness of still possessing youth and beauty afforded her a certain comfort. Hope gently whispered to her : " You can still change it ! you are still young and desirable! you will yet find a man to appreciate you and to give you the happiness which the other destroyed!"

Gradually there crept into her embittered soul envy of the youth and beauty of others and augmented the poison of her depression. There was no longer any escape from this labyrinth of woes! In whatever direction she looked, she saw only grey clouds; everywhere she saw dark and confused roads losing themselves in the darkness of a ruined life. One would suppose that by this time she would have resolutely determined to end her sufferings and remove herself from a world which had nothing more to offer her.

One who supposes any such thing is not acquainted with this type of person. He has not yet discovered the secret of "sweet sorrow," the delights of self-pity. This woman, too, found her pleasure in the tragic role which life had temporarily assigned her and to which she was clinging spasmodically with all her power. She virtually drank herself drunk with the thought that she was the unhappiest woman in the world. She directed over her own wounds all the streams of love that flowed from her warm heart. She tore these wounds open again and again so as to be unhappy and pity herself. If it did not sound so paradoxical, I would say that this woman would be unhappy if one deprived her of her unhappiness. I wonder whether an unconscious religious motive did not play a role in this self-assumed suffering. Did she hope for compensation in the life to come for all the happiness that she had missed in this world? Was her everlasting looking backwards only a voluntarily maintained attitude behind which was concealed the anticipation of never-ending looking into a radiant eternity?

All my attempts to restore her to an active life failed. The surest of all therapeutic remedies, work, failed because she never took the matter seriously. She stubbornly maintained herself in the position of looking backward, and from this position no power on earth could move her . . .

One who looks upon the Bible as a poetic account of eternal conflicts and has learned to recognise the symbolic significance of legendary lore will have no difficulty in recognizing in the story of Sodom and Gomorrah the significance of looking backwards. The woman who was converted into a pillar of salt because she looked back into the burning city—what a wonderful symbolisation of losing oneself in the past! Everyone has his secret Sodom, his Gomorrah, his disappointments, his defeats, his fearful judgments! Woe to him who looks back into the dangerous moments of his life! And does not one of von Schwab's legends warn us against the dangers of past terrors? Does it not tell us that we are flying madly over abysses, that the perils of the road are concealed and that it is dangerous to retain in the mind's eye the perils that are past?

There will be no difficulty now in comprehending my formula that to be well is to have overcome one's past. I know of no better means of distinguishing the neurotic from the healthy. The healthy person also suffers disappointments —who can escape them ?—he too suffers many a fall when he thinks he is rushing on to victory, but he will raise the tattered flag of hope and continue on his way to the assured goal. The neurotic does not get done with his past. All experiences have a tenfold seriousness for him. Whereas the healthy person throws off the burden of past disappointments, and occasionally even transforms the recollection of them to sources of pleasure, and is stimulated to new efforts by the contrasts between the pleasureable present and the sad past, the nervous person includes in his burdensome present the difficulties of the past. His memories become more and more oppressive from year to year.

It is for all the world as if the neurotic's soul were covered over with some dangerous adhesive material. Everything sticks to it and does not permit itself to be loosed from it, becomes organically united to it, wraps itself up in it, blinds his clear vision and cripples his freedom of motion. This not getting done with the past betrays itself also in his inability to forgive, in his craving for revenge and in his resentments. A neurotic is capable of reproaching one for some trifling humiliation or for some unconsidered word many years after the event. He treasures up these humiliations and defeats and does not lose sight of them for a single day. It might almost be said that he enacts daily the whole repertoire of the past.

How often are we amazed to find people who continue to make the same mistakes over and over again and whom experience seems never to teach anything. Nietzsche says: "If one has character he has his experience which keeps on recurring." In reality all that life is capable of depends upon this ability to forget the past. Of course some experiences continue to live as lessons and warnings and go to make up that uncertain treasure which we call Experience. True greatness, however, shows itself in being able to act in spite of one's experiences, in overcoming latent mistrust.

What would become of us if all of us permitted our unhappy experiences to operate as inhibitions! We should resemble a person who avoided an article of diet because it had once disagreed with him. Experience may be that which no one can learn unless one has been born with it: to find the appropriate mean from one's experiences and one's inclinations.

The nervous individual becomes useless as far as life is concerned because his experience becomes a source of doubt for him and intensifies his wanting will-power. In the presence of a new task he takes his past into consideration and makes his unhappy experiences serve as warnings, hesitates, vacillates, weighs, and finally does nothing. How much could any of us do if we lacked the courage to venture? What could we accomplish if we never thought the game worth the candle? I have often been enabled to prove that the neurotic's will is weak because his will is divided. I must supplement this with the statement that his will is oppressed by the burden of his past.

Let us after this disgression turn back to the unhappy woman with whom we began. I intimated that it was within her power to alter her destiny. Virile and kindly disposed men offered her a helping hand. But her unhappy experience begot a fear of a second disillusionment. She preferred to be unhappy rather than to venture a second time and again be unhappy.

But it is not only our past unhappiness that is dangerous. Past happiness, too, must be overcome and grow pale. Who does not know persons who are ever speaking of the past, the good old days that never return? This is a particularly striking phenomenon with reference to childhood. Some people do not seem to be capable of forgetting their blissful childhood. There is an important hint here for parents and educators who wish to assure their children a beautiful childhood. One must be careful that it is not made too beautiful! Because of the pleasureable initiation into life the later disharmonies prove too painful and awaken a longing for childhood which can be fulfilled only in fruitless dreams!

Recollections must not be permitted to kill the present. We must not be permitted to be ever lured back into the past and forever to be making comparisons. Every one of us carries the key to his past about in his bosom and opens the secret portals in order to roam about in it during the night in his dreams. In the morning, just before awaking, he locks the shrine and his daily duties resume their career. But there are people who cannot tear themselves away from their dreams and are ever harkening back to the voices of the past.

In insanity this absorption in one's past may easily be observed. The invalids become children again, with all their failings, their childish prattle, their childish pranks, and their childish games. They have come upon the road to childhood and lost the way so that they cannot get back again into the world of the grown-ups. They have looked backwards so long that finally they went backwards.

This "return to childhood" may also be observed in nervous people who have retained their critical faculty. I recall a woman of forty who employed a maid to dress and undress her, also to wash her, and who did not perform certain personal functions without the company and assistance of the maid. And I must not forget to mention the twenty-four-year-old youth who was brought to me by his mother because he was incapable of doing any work and who was not ashamed in my presence to take a good swallow of milk every five minutes from an ordinary baby's milk-bottle. This kind of "infantilism" often attains grotesque proportions. To-day the aforementioned woman laughs at the "incomprehensible malady," and the grown-up suckling is an industrious official who supports his family very comfortably. Both of them wished to defeat nature and return to childhood. Not infrequently a bodily change accompanies this mental state. The hair falls out, the features become softer, and the signs of adult masculinity undergo regressive changes. In all probability this condition is associated with certain disturbances of the internal metabolism. But who can say positively whether the impulse to these disturbances did not proceed from the stubborn look backwards, the yearning for childhood, and the enraptured glance into the depths of the past?

All the wisdom of life consists in the manner of our forgetting. What fine overtones of the harmonies and discords of the past must accompany the concords of the day! But every day has a right to its melody. Each one lives its own life and is a preparation for the future. One who fills his day with the delights and the pains of the past murders it. Only on appropriate occasions may we, must we, direct our eyes backwards, survey the path we have traversed, and again concentrate our gaze on the milestones of memory.

All ye who are ever bewailing your lot and are

incapable of rising above your fate—hearken unto me and know that ye no longer live, that ye died ere the law of destruction robbed ye of life! Let me tell ye what ye may find writ in burning letters in the firmament of knowledge: *it is never too late!* Only he has lost his life who thinks he has lost it. Forgive and forget! Drink of the lethe of work and solicitude for others! Ye are egoists! For even the mirror of your woes on which your eyes are riveted shows you only your own agonized image. And measure your pains by the infinity of pain that fills the world.

ALL-SOULS.

I am not crying for the dead who have died but who are still alive for me. I am crying for the dead who are still alive but who are dead for me. When I look back upon the long succession of years that I have travelled, and think of all my lovers who accompanied me part of the way, and then left me to wander alone, I feel as if a heavy fog were enveloping everything that otherwise appears beautiful and delightful . . .

But the dead have clung to me. They live with me, feel with me, and speak to me. When the noise of the day dies out and when the bells within begin to ring, when shapeless forms emerge from the unconscious with strange questions and uncanny gestures, when I turn from the world of reality into that of mystery, then my dead friends are with me and I hold converse with them. With every question I wish I had asked another, and I get the conviction that this other one would have answered my question, or, that other one would have understood me.

Ah! there is really so little that we desire: we wish to be understood, and do not know that we are demanding the impossible, the unattainable. For we must know ourselves ere others can comprehend us. But the urge to share ourselves with another, the longing for a heart attuned to ours deceives us as to our own inadequacy. What we do not possess we would find in another. And we compress all our stupid cravings into the one wish which appears to us as the wish for friendship.

Frightful is the thought how many friends I have lost, how many persons whom I had once thought so valuable and unreplaceable have died as far as I am concerned. And even more painful is the thought that this is the experience of all of us. Every one of us finds persons who accompany us a short distance, their hands in ours, their arms about us lovingly, and we think this will continue for ever, and then we come to a turn in the road and they have vanished. Or they travel along a road that seems to run very near our own. So near one another do we travel that we can almost touch hands even though our paths are not the same. And gradually our paths diverge. We are still within sight of one another. We can still converse with one another. Then this, too, becomes impossible. If we shout we may make ourselves heard on the other highway, but there is no reply. They are gone!

First, there were the friends of our childhood! Among these there were some whom we termed friends but who were really only a plaything, like the rocking-horse and the wooden sword. They were created only for the purpose of playing a role in the rich world of our fantasies. There was something impersonal about our friend—he did not yet cling to us. Mother used to say to us: "To-day you have a new friend!" And we were ready to accept him as such at once unless he was unsympathetic to us or obstinate or inclined to lord it over us. Of course no one could be forced on us, no matter how earnestly mother demanded it. Gradually there developed in us that dark and puzzling concept, made up of the fusion of numerous primary impulses, which we call "friendship."

Then one came along who was more to us than all the others. In his presence life was much more beautiful and richer than we had supposed; when he was absent we longed for him. When he came all our pains were forgotten. Ah, what great loves and hatreds we were capable of in the blessed era of our first friendship!

It is incomprehensible to me that I have lost the friend of my early youth. On one occasion our teachers interfered and separated us. Why they did so I do not know. But I was a wild, unruly youngster; they may have feared that by my example I might poison the inexperienced soul of my friend. But of what avail were prohibitions in the presence of our great friendship! We met secretly behind dark hedges, where no teacher's eyes could discover us. As evening approached we roamed out upon the meadow beyond the city, as far as the cemetery wall upon the gentle slope of the mountain, where we could lie down at our ease and gaze up at the stars, while we discussed the many serious questions which were beginning to trouble the souls of the maturing youngsters. When night came and wrapped the white buildings and the green gardens in a dark veil, and when the distant trumpet summoned the soldiers to their barracks, and at the sound there sprang from many an obscure nook frightened couples who quickly embraced again and said hurried farewells, we grasped each other's hands feverishly, and it seemed as if we could never, never be separated. Once we were angry at each other. It had been a serious dispute. Both of us were obstinate, for months we sulked and did not speak to each other. But one day my friend's heart melted. He confessed that he had suffered the tortures of jealousy, and that he made up only because he feared he might lose me for ever.

He was quite right. Slowly I had become half a man. Instinctively I had found among the High School pupils one who had my own inclinations, who spent sleepless nights with me in measuring verses on our fingers, fearing we might be too late for immortality. If it was the sensuous that had to be disposed of formerly, it was now the supersensuous that forced itself between the innocent pleasures of life. Now we could sit in the moonlight for hours speculating on the mysteries of existence, infinity, and immortality. Every time we discovered something beautiful we were happy for days thereafter.

He was not our only friend in those days of youthful enthusiasms. Then we had many, many friends. And when we sat in the close cafés and with palpitating hearts sang the old student-songs, and the pitcher filled with beer was passed around, we spoke of "eternal friendship" and "eternal loyalty." The "eternal" pledge was sealed by the shaking of hands, and we really felt like brothers. Every one had his good qualities which were admired, his weaknesses which were smiled at indulgently, and his strength which was feared. Each one seemed unreplaceable, and once when death snatched one of our friends from our midst we all cried like little children who want their mother.

And when we scattered in the directions of the winds, one going to the High School, the second into the army, the third into a vocation, our passion flared up again, and we swore to come together again after a certain number of years had gone by. What merry, spirited, and lusty boys we were! . . .

If only I had not seen them again, these friends! If only they could have continued to live in my memory as a precious heritage from a period that was rich in hopes and poor in disillusionments. It is with a shudder that I recall the evening, when, after many years of separation, we had a re-union. Were these my living friends ? No, these had been dead many years. I sat among corpses, among alien corpses who spoke a language that was not mine. One whom fortune had made a millionaire sat there vain and self-conscious. Absorbed in himself and morose sat one who clung to his grandiose fantasies in the modest station he occupied. A third kept looking at his watch uneasily because he had promised his wife to be home before ten o'clock. The fourth stroked his paunch and was absorbed in the mysteries of the menu. A fifth gazed at his highly-polished finger-nails and yawned. The sixth and the seventh—but enough ! They looked at one another strangely, and on the lips of all was the unuttered question : "Why in —did we come here ? "

These were friendships which had been made when we were still in our childhood. Later on the matter was not quite so simple, and it took a long time before we found one with whom we could become as one. In reality, we are still like children. We want to find a playmate for our thoughts and feelings. We let each other speak and we listen, and we call that "being understood." That is not so easy as one would like to believe. There are people who cannot listen and people to whom we cannot listen. But ultimately one finds the right person, one to whom we can entrust our secrets, one with whom we share our joys and our woes. But for how long? How strange! The fate of these friendships is sealed the moment a third person acquires the right to participate: a woman. Marriage is the rock on which most friendships split. What was formerly a question for two is now a question for three. And if the friend too marries it becomes a question for four. But how difficult it is to find four persons whose hearts beat harmoniously! What new elements now enter into the previous requirements "to understand each other!" Vanity, jealousy, envy, disfavour.

And thus we lose one friend after the other. And one day we find ourselves in an all-souls' mood, and place wreaths on the graves of the dead who are dead to us. We ask ourselves anxiously whose the fault was that we are so lonesome. And if we are not honest we blame the others. But if we are honest we see that we were not free from guilt and from all the hateful things that human beings say about one another, and we realize that it is man's destiny to be alone. The more pronounced our individuality becomes, the more sharply our qualities are outlined, the more difficult is it to lose oneself in a crowd. We are not capable of keeping our friends. We demand instead of giving. And that is why we lose them and weep at their graves.

I had one friend who was true to me through all the vicissitudes of life. Fate drove this one friend far away, and when we got the chance occasionally to see each other it was only for a few hours, which fled like seconds—so much did we have to say to each other. It was our earnest yearning once to get a chance to go away during the summer and spend a vacation together, free and unhampered, satiate ourselves with each other, and then have enough for a whole year. At the cost of many sacrifices we succeeded in having our dream fulfilled. But I would not make the attempt again. I am afraid I would lose my friend altogether.

When we found the long days before us and heard ourselves again and wanted to open our hearts to each other, we became aware—with secret horror—that we had become different in many respects. And occasionally in those beautiful hours we were conscious of something like a shudder at the thought that something fine and delicate that had been anxiously guarded might die. We separated sooner than we had planned or had originally wished. We were happy that we had parted, for we were still carrying home with us a precious heritage from our youth: our friendship—which had not yet been destroyed, but slightly bruised by rude and heavy hands. We shuddered how near we were to including ourselves among the dead.

Was that anything wonderful? Years had passed. Each one of us had experienced thousands of impressions, and what had once been common and had borne the same image had become so different that it would have been impossible to recognize them as having had a common origin. And thus it is that we stand on the roads that once were so near each other but are now so wide apart and that we call to each other like frightened children seeking flowers in the woods and longing anxiously to hear the voices of their comrades. We call to each other to prove to ourselves that we have not died.

It is all souls' day. Numberless persons are making pilgrimages to the graves of their dead to lay a flower there. I stay at home and close my eyes. I am not crying for the dead who have died but live for me. I am weeping for the dead who still live but who are dead to me. . . .

MIRROR SLAVES.

There are persons who spend their entire lives under the tyranny of the mirror. From early morning to late at night they are thinking, "How do I look to-day?" The mirror follows them into their dreams and shows them their ego horribly distorted and grotesquely transformed, or it annihilates the imperfections which make them so unhappy. Everybody has a tremendous interest in his personal appearance, an interest which may assume such proportions as to amount to self-love, to being in love with one's bodily ego, or to hatred of one's self, disgust with one's own appearance. Ultimately every one of us is egocentric. For each one of us our ego is the hub of the world. Every slightest happening is looked at and judged from the standpoint of our own ego. In the mirror slaves this trait is exaggerated to the n-th degree, to the extent of being uncanny and neurotic. They spend their lives in front of the corporeal and spiritual mirror. For they fix their gaze not only on their physical appearance, but even on their thoughts, feelings, sensations, and work; they are constantly checking themselves up, criticising themselves, and are most discontented with themselves, or they are ridicously conceited, and never cease to admire their actions and transformations.

Mirror slaves waste a part of their lives in front of the mirror. They keep a little mirror by them constantly so as to look at themselves from time to time. They can't pass a mirror without stopping in front of it long enough to survey themselves from head to foot. There is a story of a king who promised to give his daughter in marriage to the man who would pass a certain mirror without looking into it. Vanity foiled all but a poet, and the princess was awarded to him. (And, in all probability, the poet did not look into the mirror because he was absorbed in admiring his ego in the mirror of his soul!) This story teaches us the intensity of human vanity. In the case of mirror slaves this human failing becomes a disease; it fills their lives and, under certain circumstances, unfits them for life.

A mirror slave devotes a great deal of attention to the matter of his external appearance. He is dominated by an imperative which makes life a torture. This imperative is: "What will people think of me?" He feels all eyes are upon him, everybody is looking at him, everybody is thinking of his appearance. He has a horrible fear of being laughed at. For God's sake! only not to be laughed at, not to become the subject of other people's mirth! He would love to be lost in the crowd and not be noticed. If he could only possess a magic cap that would enable him to go about invisible! On the other hand he thirsts for triumphs. He would like to find favour, to be larger, bigger, more elegant and more beautiful than others, would like to shine in society, and be able to outshine others in wit, intellect, vivacity, education and culture. Above all he is desirous of making an impression on the opposite sex, to make conquests, to be a Lothario, free from all restraints, uninterfered with in his inclinations, and unconcerned about the judgment of his environment.

The mirror slave begins his day with the question, "What shall I wear to-day?" As soon as a careful inspection has convinced him that this is going to be a good or a bad day for him, that he is looking younger or older, sick or well, the painful task of selection begins. What dress will be most adapted to the tasks of this day, to the weather, or to the mood? After some deliberation a choice is made. But then, all of a sudden, the mirror discloses a blemish! Woe! The toilet must be gone all over again. Everything is weighed carefully in the balance, and finally the arduous task is completed.

And now the mirror slave's martyrdom begins. He studies the people he meets to see whether they greet him or ignore him, are friendly or unfriendly, pleased or indifferent, etc., whether they take note of him, whisper behind his back, criticise him, make remarks about him, or make merry over him. If one laughs without his participation he is on the rack; unquestionably it was he who was being laughed at: there must be something wrong with his clothes. Why is everybody looking at him so curiously? In his distress he may even be induced to address strangers. "Why did they stare at me so fixedly?" In a sudden outburst of passion he may even call an acquaintance to account for not having greeted him or for having done so carelessly.

He experiences extraordinary sensations when he puts on new articles of clothing. What a difficult task it is to go out in new shoes! All eyes must be magically directed on his shoes. He makes himself ridiculous with his new shoes. People surely think him silly or a slave of fashion. He lives through all this with every new garment, and ultimately he develops a fear of changing his clothes and goes about in old, worn, and even shabby clothing, thinking that thus he attracts less attention.

All daily tasks become a great undertaking. To go into a store to make a purchase, to enter a theatre when other spectators are already seated, or to look around for a seat in a restaurant, etc., are difficult and often impossible tasks. He loves to be the first person in the theatre or at the concert—to come in while the hall is still empty. The selection of a seat is a source of worry. A mirror slave would love to sit alone in a box or in the front row if he were not so afraid of being looked at—which is exactly what he longs for. He therefore conceals himself in a modest inconspicuous seat, but does not enjoy himself because he is always impelled to observe and study the people.

He is a slave of public opinion. At no price would he do anything not quite proper, that would cause the slightest head-shake, or would make him the subject of public comment. He would purchase the good-will of all, court everybody's favour, and wants to be loved and admired by the whole world. He spares no pains to get the approval of his environment. He is one of the eternally amiable, modest, and helpful persons that we encounter now and then. He gives very liberal tips in order that he may be highly thought of. In fact, he loves to give presents and fears nothing so much as being thought niggardly.

In time he becomes socially useless. A trivial public function, a speech, a betrothal, any appearance in public liberates a whole host of apprehensive ideas. If he happens to be an artist he fears to make a public appearance, and contents himself with being a teacher. If he overcomes his fear of appearing in public, he becomes the slave of the critics. An unfavourable criticism brings him to the verge of despair; a favourable criticism temporarily lifts him above all difficulties.

If we inquire into the cause of this neurosis we find it to be a defective educational method in childhood, which has led the child to overvalue its environment and has inplanted in it a pathologic degree of vanity. How many parents have the habit of calling the child's attention to the fact that people are looking at it, observing it, or laughing at it! How often when a child is wearing a new garment is it told that everybody is looking at it and admiring it! And how often is a child admired and worshipped to such an extent that it really imagines itself the hub of its little world! All the boundless over-valuation of the world, of one's surroundings, the striving for public recognition, for reputation, for honour emanate from our childhood years. We ought to make it our object to bring about just the opposite. The child should be brought up to be modest, to learn that happiness lies in the feeling of having done one's duty, in the quiet joys of life, in work, in a capacity for enjoyment. It is our duty to limit the child's vanity, to restrain his ambition, and to train him to be self-reliant. One who has learned to consider contentment with oneself—not self-satisfaction based on vanity and arrogance—as worth more than what people say about one has found the way to health and happiness.

Who would deny that a mirror has its uses? Who does not know that it is necessary occasionally to observe ourselves in the mirror of the body and the soul so that we may recognize our shortcomings, remove our blemishes, and make ourselves better and more beautiful? All excess becomes a vice. A mirror is a dangerous thing for the vain person who cannot live without it. Everything is a mirror to him. The world as a whole is a mirrored salon which reflects his image from every point. But he fails to see that behind these mirrors there is another world to which he has lost access. For the next step beyond this mirror-neurosis is insanity, a disease which we now know is a losing of oneself in oneself.

Printed in Great Britain by The Cheltenham Press, Cheltenham, Glos.

For Product Safety Concerns and Information please contact our EU
representative GPSR@taylorandfrancis.com
Taylor & Francis Verlag GmbH, Kaufingerstraße 24, 80331 München, Germany

www.ingramcontent.com/pod-product-compliance
Lightning Source LLC
Chambersburg PA
CBHW061729270326
41928CB00011B/2162